Community & Growth

Our Pilgrimage Together

books by Jean Vanier
published by Paulist Press

ERUPTION TO HOPE
BE NOT AFRAID
FOLLOWERS OF JESUS

Community & Growth

Our Pilgrimage Together

by Jean Vanier

PAULIST PRESS
New York, N.Y./Ramsey, N.J.

© Jean Vanier, 1979

First published by Griffin Press Limited,
461 King Street West, Toronto M5V 1K7, Canada

The Scripture quotations in this publication are from the
Revised Standard Version Common Bible,
copyrighted © 1973.

Library of Congress
Catalog Card Number: 79-91603

ISBN: 0-8091-2294-4

Published by Paulist Press
545 Island Road, Ramsey, N.J. 07446

Printed and bound in Canada.

CONTENTS:

INTRODUCTION

At one time, men lived in homogenous groups, composed of more or less the same family, with the same roots. In these groups—the tribe, the village—people spoke the same language, lived by the same rites and traditions, had the same code of behaviour and accepted the same authority. There was a solidarity among them. This solidarity came both from their flesh and blood and from the need to cooperate to meet material needs and to defend the group from enemy attack and natural dangers. There was a unity among people of the same group which etched itself deeply on their unconscious.

Times have changed. Contemporary society is the product of the disintegration of these more or less natural or familial groupings. Nowadays, people who live in the same area are no longer part of a homogenous group. Towns are made up of neighbours who do not know each other—and this will soon be true of villages, too. People are afraid, and so shut themselves up in their own houses. Human community is no longer to be found in the street, the neighbourhood or the village. Mobility has brought a mixture of people, religions and philosophies.

This state of things brings a loneliness which people have more or less difficulty in coping with. The family, sometimes shrunk to just a couple and their children, can no longer be self-sufficient. It seeks out friends. People cannot live as if they were on a desert island. They need companions, friends with whom they can share their lives, their vision and their ideals. So it is that people come together, not because they live in the same neighbourhood or are related, but because of a mutual sympathy; they come together around ideas, around a vision of man and society, a common interest. Some of them meet occasionally. Others decide to live under the same roof: they leave their own neighbourhoods and relations, sometimes their work as well, to live with others in a community based on these new criteria and this new vision.

At the same time, they want to bear witness to those values. They feel that they have some good news to offer the world, news which brings greater happiness, truth and fulfillment. They want to become the yeast in the dough of human society. They want to work for peace and justice among all men and all nations.

Some of these groupings are geared to action, to a specific task or struggle. Their members live together not as brothers and sisters, but as working and fighting comrades. They pool their capacity for action. Other groupings are more geared to a way of life, to the quality of relationships among their members and to welcome than to action. Their "action" is witnessing to their life and their welcome. These are the two poles of community: the goal which attracts and unites, the centre of interest which provides the "why" of life together; and the friendship which binds people, the sense of belonging to a group, solidarity and personal relationships.

In fact, there is a multiplicity of goals, just as there are many ways of translating a sense of solidarity and belonging. When I use the word "community" in this book, I am talking essentially of groupings of people who have left their own milieu to live with others under the same roof, and work from a new vision of human beings and their relationships with each other and with God. So my definition is a very restricted one. Others would see "community" as something wider.

This book is above all for those who live, or want to live, in community. But many of its points apply equally to family life. The two essential elements of life in community are also part of life in a family: inter-personal relationship and a sense of belonging, and orientation of life to a common goal and common witness. In the same way, some of the book can apply to people who, although they do not live together, are deeply bound to each other and meet regularly to share about an ideal, to pray or to work.

Almost everything I say here is the result of my own experience of life in l'Arche, the community in which I have been living for 14 years. I have also, though, learned a great deal from visiting l'Arche communities across the world and by listening to others who live in other sorts of community.

L'Arche is special, in the sense that we are trying to live in community with people who are mentally handicapped. Certainly we want to help them grow and reach the greatest independence possible. But before "doing for them", we want to "be with them." The particular suffering of the person who is mentally handicapped, as of all marginal people, is a feeling of being excluded, worthless and unloved. It is through everyday life in community and the love which must be incarnate in this, that handicapped people can begin to discover that they have a value, that they are loved and so loveable.

I began l'Arche in 1964, in the desire to live the Gospel and to follow Jesus Christ more closely. Each day brings me new lessons on how much Christian life must grow in commitment to life in community, and on how much that life needs faith, the love of Jesus and the presence of the Holy Spirit if it is to deepen. Everything I say about life in community in these pages is inspired by my faith in Jesus.

That certainly doesn't mean that there is no community life outside Christianity. To claim that would be to go against all human experience and against common sense as well. As soon as men group together, for whatever reason, a sort of community is created. But the message of Jesus invites his disciples to love one another and to live community in a special way.

Through being close to many people attracted by community and by new ways of life, I have come to realise how great an ignorance there is about community life. Many people seem to believe that creating a community is a matter of simply gathering together under the same roof a few people who get on reasonably well together or are committed to the same ideal. The result can be disasterous! Community life isn't simply created by either spontaneity or laws. Some precise conditions have to be met if this life is to deepen and grow through all the crises, tensions and "good times." If these conditions aren't met, every sort of deviation is possible; these will lead eventually to the actual or spiritual death of the community, and its members will become enslaved.

This book tries to clarify the conditions which are necessary to life in community. It is no thesis or treatise. It is made up of a series of starting-points for reflection, which I have discovered not through books, but through everyday life, through my mistakes, my set-backs and my personal failings, through the inspiration of God and my brothers and sisters, and through the moments of unity between us as well as the tension and suffering. Life in community is a marvellous adventure. My hope is that many people can live this adventure, which in the end is one of interior liberation—the freedom to love and to be loved.

> "As the Father has loved me, so have I loved you; abide in my love.
> "This is my commandment, that you love one another as I have loved you. Greater love has no man than this, that a man lay down his life for his friends."
>
> (John 15,9,12,13)

DEDICATION

To Father Thomas Philippe
with whom I made my first steps in community

ACKNOWLEDGEMENT

I wrote this book in French. It was Ann Shearer, in London, who with such deep and intimate knowledge of l'Arche, translated it. She did it beautifully and I am deeply grateful to her.

Jean Vanier

1

ONE HEART, ONE SOUL, ONE SPIRIT

In these times, when towns are depersonalised and depersonalising, many people are looking for community, especially when they feel alone, tired, weak and unhappy. Some people find it impossible to be alone; for them, this is a foretaste of death. So community can appear to be a marvellously welcoming and sharing place.

But in another way, community is a terrible place. It is the place where our limitations and our egoism are revealed to us. When we begin to live full-time with others, we discover our poverty and our weaknesses, our inability to get on with people, our mental and emotional blocks, our affective or sexual disturbances, our seemingly insatiable desires, our frustrations and jealousies, our hatred and our wish to destroy. While we were alone, we could believe we loved everyone. Now that we are with others, we realise how incapable we are of loving, how much we deny life to others. And if we become incapable of loving, what is left? There is nothing but blackness, despair and anguish. Love seems an illusion. We seem to be condemned to solitude and death.

So community life brings a painful revelation of our limitations, weaknesses and darkness; the unexpected discovery of the monsters within us is hard to accept. The immediate reaction is to try to destroy the monsters, or to hide them away again, pretending that they don't exist, or to flee from community life and relationships with others, or to find that the monsters are theirs, not ours. But if we accept that the monsters are there, we can let them out and learn to tame them. That is growth towards liberation.

If we are accepted with our limitations as well as our abilities, community gradually becomes a place of liberation. Discovering that we are accepted and loved by others, we are better able to accept and love ourselves. So community is the place where we can be ourselves without fear or constraint. Community life deepens through mutual trust among all its members.

So this terrible place can become one of life and growth. There is nothing more beautiful than a community where people are beginning really to love and trust each other. "Behold, how good and pleasant it is when brothers dwell in unity! It is like the precious oil upon the head, running down upon the beard, upon the beard of Aaron. . . . " (Psalm 133).

I have never understood this reference to Aaron's beard very well—probably because I don't have a beard myself. But if oil running down a beard brings as amazing a feeling as life in community, then it must be marvellous!

* * *

In community life we discover our own deepest wound and learn to accept it. So our rebirth can begin. It is from this very wound that we are born.

* * *

The sense of belonging

When I visit African villages, I realise that through their rituals and traditions they are deeply living community life. Each person has a sense of belonging to the others; men of the same ethnic origin or village are truly brothers. I remember Mgr. Agré, Bishop of Man, meeting a customs officer at Abidjan airport; they embraced like brothers because they came from the same village, they belonged to each other in some way. Most Africans don't need to talk about community. They live it intensely.

I've heard that Aborigines in Australia buy nothing except cars, which enable them to visit their clan. The only thing they find important is this link of brotherhood, which they cherish. There is, it seems, such a unity between them that they know when one of them is dying; they feel it in their guts.

Rene Lenoir, in _Les Exclus_,[1] says that if a prize is offered

[1] Le Seuil, Paris 1974

2

for the first to answer a question in a group of Canadian Indian children, they all work out the answer together and shout it out at the same time. They couldn't bear one to win, leaving the rest of them losers. The winner would be separated from his brothers; he would have won the prize but lost solidarity.

Our Western civilisation is competitive. From the time they start school, children learn to "win." Their parents are delighted when they come first in class. This is how individualistic material progress and the desire to gain prestige by coming out on top have taken over from the sense of fellowship, compassion and community. Now people live more or less on their own in a small house, jealously guarding their goods and planning to acquire more, with a notice on the gate that says "Beware of the Dog." It is because the West has lost its sense of community that small groups are springing up here and there, trying to refind it.

We have a lot to learn from the African and the Indian. They remind us that the essence of community is a sense of belonging. Of course their sense of community can get in the way of their seeing others objectively and lovingly. That is how tribal wars begin. Sometimes too African community life is based on fear. The group or the tribe give life and a sense of solidarity; they protect and offer security, but they are not really liberating. If people cut themselves off from the group, they are alone with their fears and their own deep wound, facing evil forces, wicked spirits and death. These fears are expressed in rites or fetishes, which in turn are a force for cohesion. True community is liberating.

* * *

I love that passage from the Bible: "And I will say...'You are my people'; and he shall say 'Thou art my God'" (Hosea 2,23).

I shall always remember Jessie Jackson, one of Martin Luther King's disciples, saying to a gathering of many thousands of blacks: "My people are humiliated." Mother Theresa of Calcutta says, "My people are hungry."

"My people" are my community, which is both the small community, those who live together, and the larger community which surrounds it and for which it is there. "My people" are

3

those who are written in my flesh as I am in theirs. Whether we are near each other or far away, my brothers and sisters remain written within me. I carry them, and they, me; we know each other again when we meet. To call them "my people" doesn't mean that I feel superior to them, or that I am their shepherd or that I look after them. It means that they are mine as I am theirs. There is a solidarity between us. What touches them, touches me. And when I say "my people", I don't imply that there are others I reject. My people is my community, made up of those who know me and carry me. They are a springboard towards all humanity. I cannot be a universal brother unless I first love my people.

* * *

The longer we journey on the road to unity, the more the sense of belonging grows and deepens. The sense is not just one of belonging to a community. It is a sense of belonging to the universe, to the earth, to the air, to the water, to everything that lives, to all humanity. If the community gives a sense of belonging, it also helps us to accept our aloneness in a personal meeting with God. Through this, the community is open to the universe and to mankind.

* * *

Towards the goals of community

A community must have a project of some kind. If people decide to live together with neither specific goals nor clarity about the "why" of their common life, there will soon be conflicts and the whole thing will collapse. Tensions in community often come from the fact that individuals have not talked about their expectations. They quickly discover that each of them wants something very different. I imagine that the same thing can happen in marriage. It is not simply a question of wanting to live together. If the marriage is to last, you have to know what you want to do and to be together.

This means that every community must have a Charter, which specifies clearly why its members are living together and what is expected of each of them. It also means that before a community begins, its members should take time to prepare for living together and clarify their aims.

4

Bruno Bettleheim has said:[1]

"I am convinced communal life can flourish only if it exists for an aim outside itself. Community is viable if it is the outgrowth of a deep involvement in a purpose which is other than, or above, that of being a community."

The more authentic and creative a community is in its search for the essential, the more its members are called beyond their own concerns and tend to unite. The more lukewarm a community becomes towards its original goals, the more danger there is of its membership crumbling, and of tensions. Its members will no longer talk about how they can best respond to the call of God and the poor. They will talk instead about themselves and their problems, their wealth or their poverty, the structures of the community. There is a vital link between the two poles of community: its goal and the unity of its members.

* * *

A community becomes truly and radiantly one when all its members have a sense of urgency. There are too many people in the world who have no hope. There are too many cries which go unheard. There are too many people dying in loneliness. It is when the members of a community realise that they are not there simply for themselves or their own sanctification, but to welcome the gift of God, to hasten His Kingdom and to quench the thirst in parched hearts, that they will truly live community. A community must be a light in a world of darkness, a spring of fresh water in the church and for all men. We have no right to become lukewarm.

* * *

From "the community for myself" to "myself for the community"

A community is only a community when the majority of its members is making the transition from "the community for myself" to "myself for the community", when each person's heart is opening to all the others, without any exception. This is the movement from egoism to love, from death to resurrection; it is the Easter, the passover of the Lord. It is also the

[1] *Home for the Heart*, Thames and Hudson, London, 1974

5

passing from a land of slavery to a promised land, the land of interior freedom.

A community isn't just a place where people live under the same roof; that is a lodging house or an hotel. Nor is a community a work-team. Even less is it a nest of vipers! It is a place where everyone—or, let's be realistic, the majority!—is emerging from the shadows of egocentricity to the light of a real love.

> "Do nothing from selfishness or conceit, but in humility count others better than yourselves. Let each of you look not only to his own interests, but also to the interests of others."
>
> (Philippians 2,3-4)

Love is neither sentimental nor a passing emotion. It is an attraction to others which gradually becomes commitment, the recognition of a covenant, of a mutual belonging. It is listening to others, being concerned for them and feeling empathy with them. It means answering their call and their deepest needs. It means feeling and suffering with them—weeping when they weep, rejoicing when they rejoice. Loving people means being happy when they are there, sad when they are not. It is living in each other, taking refuge in each other. "Love is a power for unity", says Denys l'Areopage. And if love means moving towards each other, it also and above all means moving together in the same direction, hoping and wishing for the same things. Love means sharing the same vision and the same ideal. So it means wanting others to fulfil themselves, according to God's plan and in service to other people. It means wanting them to be faithful to their own calling, free to love in all the dimensions of their being.

There we have the two poles of community: a sense of belonging to each other and a desire that each of us goes further in our own gift to God and to others, a desire that there is more light in us, and a deeper truth and peace.

> "Love is patient and kind; love is not jealous or boastful; it is not arrogant or rude. Love does not insist on its own way; it is not irritable or resentful; it does not rejoice at wrong, but rejoices in the right. Love bears all things, believes all things, hopes all things, endures all things."
>
> (I Corinthians 13,4-7)

It takes time for a heart to make this passage from egoism to love, from "the community for myself" to "myself for the community", and the community for God and those in need. It takes time and much purification, and constant deaths which bring new resurrections. To love, we must die continually to our own ideas, our own susceptibilities and our own comfort. The path of love is woven of sacrifice. The roots of egoism are deep in our unconscious; our first reactions of self-defence, aggression and the search for personal gratification often grow from them.

Loving is not only a voluntary act which involves controlling and overcoming our own sensibilities—that is just the beginning. It also demands a purified heart and feelings which go out spontaneously to the other. These deep purifications can only come through a gift of God, a grace which springs from the deepest part of ourselves, where the Holy Spirit lives. "I will give them one heart and put a new spirit within them; I will take the stony heart out of their flesh, and give them a heart of flesh" (Ezekiel II;19). Jesus has promised to send us the Holy Spirit, the Paraclete, to infuse us with this new energy, this strength, this quality of heart which will make it possible for us truly to welcome the other—even our enemy—as he or she is, possible for us to bear all things, believe all things, hope all things. Learning to love takes a lifetime, because the Holy Spirit must penetrate even the smallest corners of our being, all the places where there are fears, defences and envy.

Community begins to form when each person tries to welcome and love the others as they are.

"Welcome one another, therefore, as Christ has welcomed you."
(Romans 15,7)

* * *

Sympathies and antipathies

The two great dangers of community are "friends" and "enemies." People very quickly get together with those who are like themselves; we all like to be with someone who pleases us, who shares our ideas, ways of looking at life and sense of humour. We nourish each other, we flatter each other; "You are marvellous"—"So are you"—"We are marvellous because

7

we are intelligent and clever." Human friendships can very quickly become a club of mediocrities, enclosed in mutual flattery and approval. Friendship is then no longer a spur to go further, to be of greater service to our brothers and sisters, to be more faithful to the gifts we have been given, more attentive to the Spirit; we stop walking across the desert to the land of liberation. Friendship becomes stifling, a barrier between ourselves and others and their needs. It can become an emotional dependence which is a form of slavery.

* * *

There are also "antipathies" in community. There are always people with whom we don't agree, who block us, who contradict us and who stifle the treasure of our life and our freedom. Their presence seems menacing and brings out in us either aggression or a sort of servile regression. We seem incapable of expressing ourselves or even of living when we are with them. Others bring out our envy and jealousy; they are everything we wish we were ourselves and their presence reminds us that we are not. Their radiance and their intelligence underline our own poverty. Others ask too much of us: we cannot respond to their incessant emotional demands and we have to push them away. These are the "enemies." They endanger us, and, even if we dare not admit it, we hate them. Certainly, this is only a psychological hatred—it isn't yet a moral hatred, because it is not deliberate. But even so, we just wish these people didn't exist! If they disappeared or died, it would seem like a liberation.

These blocks as well as attractions between different personalities are natural. They come from an emotional immaturity and a whole lot of elements from our childhood over which we have no control. There can be no question of denying them.

But if we let ourselves be guided by our emotional reactions, cliques will very quickly start to form within the community. It will become no longer a community but a collection of people more or less shut in on themselves and blocked off from others. When you go into some communities, you can quickly sense these tensions and underground battles. People don't look each other in the face. They pass each other in the corridors like ships in the night. A community is only a community when the majority of its members have consciously decided to break these barriers and come out of their cocoons of "friendship" to stretch out their hand to their enemies.

But the journey is a long one. A community isn't built in a day. In fact, it is never completely finished. It is always either growing towards greater love, or regressing.

* * *

Our enemies frighten us. We are incapable of hearing their cries, of responding to their needs. Their aggression or domination stifles us. We flee from them—or wish that they would disappear.

In fact, we have to become aware of our own weakness, lack of maturity and inner poverty. Perhaps it is this which we refuse to look at. The faults we criticise in others are often our own which we refuse to face. Those who criticise others and the community, and seek an ideal one, are often in flight from their own flaws and weaknesses. They refuse to accept their own feeling of dissatisfaction, their own wound.

The message of Jesus is clear: "But I say to you that hear, love your enemies, do good to those who hate you, bless those who curse you, pray for those who abuse you. To him who strikes you on the cheek, offer the other also ... If you love those who love you, what credit is that to you? For even sinners love those who love them" (Luke 6,27-9,32).

* * *

False friends are the ones in whom we see only good qualities. They bring out a vitality and feeling of well-being in us. They reveal us to ourselves and we find them stimulating. That is why we love them. The enemy, by contrast, brings out emotions in us that we don't want to look at: aggression, envy, fear, false dependence, hatred—the whole dark world within us.

As long as we refuse to accept that we are a mixture of light and darkness, of positive qualities and failings, of love and hate, of altruism and egocentricity, of maturity and immaturity, we will continue to divide the world into enemies—the "baddies"—and friends—"the goodies." We will go on throwing up barriers within and around ourselves and spreading prejudice.

When we accept that we have weaknesses and flaws, but that we can still grow towards interior freedom and truer love, then we can accept the weaknesses and flaws of others, who can also grow towards the freedom of love; we can look at all men and women with realism and love. We are all mortal and fragile. But we have a hope, because it is possible to grow.

* * *

Forgiveness at the heart of community

Is it possible, though, to accept ourselves, with our darkness, weaknesses, flaws and fear, without the revelation that God loves us? It is when we discover that the Father sent his only beloved son not to judge us, not to condemn, but to heal, save and guide us on the paths of love, and to forgive us because he loves us in the depths of our being, that we can accept ourselves. There is hope. We are not imprisoned for ever by egoism and darkness. It is possible to love.

So it becomes possible to accept others and to forgive.

* * *

As long as we see in the other only those qualities which reflect our own, no growth is possible; the relationship remains static and sooner or later will end. A relationship is only authentic and stable when it is founded on the acceptance of weakness, on forgiveness and on the hope of growth.

If community reaches its height in celebration, its heart is forgiveness.

* * *

Community is the place of forgiveness. In spite of all the trust we may have in each other, there are always words that wound, self-promoting attitudes, situations where susceptibilities clash. That is why living together implies a certain cross, a constant effort and an acceptance which is daily and mutual forgiveness. Saint Paul says:

> "Put on then, as God's chosen ones, holy and beloved, compassion, kindness, lowliness, meekness and patience, forbearing one another and, if one has a complaint against another, forgiving each other; as the Lord has forgiven you, so you also must forgive. And above all these put on love, which binds everything together in perfect harmony. And let the peace of Christ rule in your hearts, to which indeed you were called in the one body. And be thankful."
>
> (Colossians 3,12-15)

Too many people come into community to find something,

to belong to a dynamic group, to find a life which approaches the ideal. If we come into community without knowing that the reason we come is to discover the mystery of forgiveness, we will soon be disappointed.

* * *

Have patience

We are not the masters of our own feelings of attraction or revulsion, which come from the places in ourselves over which we have little or no control. All we can do is try not to follow inclinations which make for barriers within the community. We have to hope that the Holy Spirit will come to forgive, purify and trim the rather twisted branches of our being. Our emotional makeup has grown from a thousand fears and egoisms since our infancy, as well as from signs of love and the gift of God. It is a mixture of shadow and light. And so it will not be straightened out in a day; this will take a thousand purifications and pardons, daily efforts and above all a gift of the Holy Spirit which renews us from within.

* * *

It is a long haul to transform our emotional makeup so that we can start really loving our enemy. We have to be patient with our feelings and fears; we have to be merciful to ourselves. If we are to make the passage to acceptance and love of the other—all the others—we must start very simply, by recognising our own blocks, jealousies, ways of comparing ourselves to others, prejudices and hatreds. We have to recognise that we are poor creatures, that we are what we are. And we have to ask our Father to forgive us. It is good, then, to speak to a priest or a man of God who perhaps could help us to understand what is happening, strengthen us in our efforts and help us discover God's pardon.

Once we have recognised that a branch is twisted, that we have these blocks of antipathy, the next step is to try to be careful of how we speak. We have to try to hold our tongue, which can so quickly sow discord, which likes to spread the faults and mistakes of others, which rejoices when it can prove someone wrong. The tongue is one of the smallest parts of our body, but it can sow death. We are quick to magnify the faults of others, just to hide our own. It is so often "they" who are wrong. When we accept our own flaws, it is easier to accept those of others.

* * *

At the same time, we should try loyally to see the good qualities of our enemies. After all, they must have a few! But because we are afraid of them, perhaps they are afraid of us. If we have blocks, they too must have them. It is hard for two people who are afraid of each other to discover their mutual qualities. They need a mediator, a conciliator, an artisan of peace, someone in whom both have confidence. This third person can perhaps help us to discover the qualities of our enemy, or at least to understand our own attitudes and blocks. When we have seen the enemy's qualities, one day we will be able to use our tongue to say something good about him. It is a long journey, which will end the day we can ask our former "enemy" for advice or a favour. We all find it far more touching to be asked to help than we do to be helped or "done good to."

Throughout this time, the Holy Spirit can help us to pray for our enemies, to pray that they too grow as God would have them grow, so that one day the reconciliation may be made. Perhaps one day the Holy Spirit will liberate us from this block of antipathy. Perhaps He will let us go on walking with this thorn in our flesh—this thorn which humiliates us and forces us to renew our efforts each day. We shouldn't get worried about our bad feelings. Still less should we feel guilty. We should ask God's forgiveness, like little children, and keep on walking. We shouldn't get discouraged if the road is long. One of the roles of community life is precisely to keep us walking in hope, to help us accept ourselves as we are and others as they are.

Patience, like forgiveness, is at the heart of community life— patience with ourselves and the laws of our own growth, and patience with others. The hope of a community is founded on the acceptance and love of ourselves and others as we really are, and on the patience and trust which is essential to growth.

* * *

Mutual trust

The mutual trust at the heart of community is born of each day's forgiveness and the acceptance of our frailty and poverty.

12

But this trust is not developed overnight. That is why it takes time to form a real community. When people join a community, they always present a certain image of themselves because they want to conform to what the others expect of them. Gradually, they discover that the others love them as they are and trust them. But this trust must stand the test and must always be growing.

Newly-married couples may love each other a great deal. But there may be something superficial in this love, which has to do with the excitement of discovery. Love is even deeper between people who have been married for a long time, who have lived through difficulties together and who know that the other will be faithful until death. They know that nothing can break their union.

It is the same in our communities. It is often after suffering, after very great trials, tensions and the proof of fidelity that trust grows. A community in which there is truly mutual trust is a community which is indestructable.

* * *

So a community is not simply a group of people who love together and love each other. It is a current of life, a heart, a soul, a spirit. It is people who love each other a great deal and who are all reaching towards the same hope. This is what brings the special atmosphere of joy and welcome which characterises the true community.

> "So if there is any encouragement in Christ, any incentive of love, any participation in the Spirit, any affection and sympathy, complete my joy by being of the same mind, having the same love, being in full accord and of one mind."
>
> (Philippians 2;1-2)
>
> "Now the company of those who believed were of one heart and soul, and no one said that any of the things which he possessed was his own, but they had everything in common."
>
> (Acts 4; 32)

This atmosphere of joy comes from the fact that we all feel free to be ourselves in the deepest sense. We have no need to play a role, to pretend to be better than the others, to demonstrate prowess in order to be loved. We have discovered that we are loved for ourselves, not for our intellectual or manual skills.

When we begin to drop the barriers and fears which prevent us from being ourselves, we become more simple. Simplicity is no more and no less than being ourselves. It is knowing that we are accepted with our qualities, our flaws and as we most deeply are.

* * *

I am becoming more and more aware that the great difficulty of many of us who live in community is that we lack self-confidence,. We can so quickly feel that we are not really loveable, that if others saw us as we really were, they would reject us. We are afraid of all this is darkness in ourselves; we are afraid to face our emotional or sexual problems; we are afraid that we are incapable of real love. We swing so quickly from exhilaration to depression, and neither expresses what we really are. How can we become convinced that we are loved in our poverty and weakness and that we too are capable of loving?

That is the secret of growth in community. It comes from a gift of God which may pass through others. As we discover gradually that God and the others trust us, it becomes a little easier for us to trust ourselves, and in turn to trust others.

* * *

To live in community is to discover and love the secret of what is unique in ourselves. This is how we become free. Then we no longer live according to the desires of others, or by an image of ourselves; we become free to discover the essence of the other.

* * *

The right to be oneself

I have always wanted to write a book called *The Right to be a Rotter*. A fairer title is perhaps, *The Right to be Oneself.* One of the great difficulties of community life is that we sometimes force people to be what they are not: we stick an ideal image on them to which they are obliged to conform. If they don't manage to live up to this image, they become afraid that they won't be loved, or that they will disappoint others. If they do live up to the image, then they think they are perfect. But community is not about perfect people. It is about people who are bound to each other, each of whom is their own mixture of good and bad, darkness and light, love and hate. And community is the only earth in which each of them can grow without fear towards the liberation of the forces of love which are hidden in them. But there can only be growth if we recognise the potential; and so there are many things in us to be purified—there are shadows to turn into light and fears to turn into trust.

Often we expect too much of people in community life. We prevent them from discovering and accepting themselves as they are. We are so quick to judge them or to put them into categories. So they feel obliged to hide behind a mask. But they have the right to be rotters, to have their own dark places, and corners of envy and even hatred in their hearts. These jealousies and insecurities are natural; they aren't any kind of "shameful disease." They are part of our wounded nature. That is our reality. We have to learn to accept them and to live with them without drama, and to walk towards liberation, gradually knowing ourselves to be forgiven.

Some people in community, it seems to me, live a sort of unconscious guilt; they feel that they are not what they should be. They need to be affirmed and encouraged to trust. They must feel able to share even their weaknesses without the risk of rejection.

* * *

There is a part of each of us which is already luminous, already converted. And there is a part which is still in shadow. A community is not made up only of the converted. It is made up of all the elements in us which need to be transformed, purified and pruned. It is made up also of the "unconverted."

* * *

There are people in community with very deep psychological wounds, who carry real blocks and serious neuroses. They were terribly bruised in their childhood; they have had to build huge barriers because of their vulnerability. They don't always need to be sent to a psychiatrist, nor to be given psychotherapy. Many people are called to live all their lives with these blocks and barriers. They too are children of God and God can work through and with them, and with their neuroses, for the good of the community. They too have their gift to offer. Don't let's "psychiatrise" things too much. Through the forgiveness of each day, let us help each other to accept these neuroses and barriers.

Anyway, that's the best way to dissolve them!

* * *

Called together just as we are

God seems pleased to call together in Christian communities people who, humanly speaking, are very different, who come from very different cultures, classes and countries. The most beautiful communities are created from just this diversity of people and temperaments. This means that each person must love the others with all their differences, and work with them for the community.

These people would never have chosen to live with each other. Humanly speaking, it seems an impossible challenge. But it is precisely because it is impossible that they have an inner conviction that God has chosen them to live in this community. And so the impossible becomes possible. They no longer rely on their own human abilities or natural sympathies, but on their Father who has called them to live together. He will give them the new heart and spirit which will enable them all to become witnesses to love. In fact, the more impossible it is in human terms, the more of a sign it is that their love comes from God and that Jesus is living: "By this all men will know that you are my disciples, if you have love for one another" (John 13,35).

* * *

When he created the first community of the apostles, Jesus chose to live with men who were very different from one another: Peter, Matthew (the publican), Simon (the Zealot), Judas, and so on. They would never have come together if their Master had not called them.

* * *

We shouldn't seek the ideal community. It is a question of loving those whom God has set beside us today. They are signs of God. We might have chosen different people, people who were more cheerful and intelligent. But these are the ones God has given given us, the ones He has chosen for us. It is with them that we are called to create unity and live a covenant.

* * *

16

I am more and more struck by people in community who are dissatisfied. When they live in small communities, they want to be in larger ones, where there is more nourishment, where there are more community activities, or where the liturgy is more beautifully prepared. And when they are in large communities, they dream of ideal small ones. Those who have a lot to do dream of having plenty of time for prayer; those who have a lot of time for themselves seem to get bored and search distractedly for some sort of activity which will give a sense to their lives. And don't we all dream of the perfect community, where we will be at peace and in complete harmony, with a perfect balance between the exterior and the interior, where everything will be joyful?

It is difficult to make people understand that the ideal doesn't exist, that personal equilibrium and the harmony they dream of come only after years and years of struggle, and that even then they come only as flashes of grace and peace. If we are always looking for our own equilibrium, I'd even say if we are looking too much for our own peace, we will never find it, because peace is the fruit of love and service to others. I'd like to tell the many people in communities who are looking for this impossible ideal: "Stop looking for peace, give yourselves where you are. Stop looking at yourselves—look instead at your brothers and sisters in need. Be close to those God has given you in community today; work with the references which God has given you today. Ask how you can better love your brothers and sisters. Then you will find peace. You will find rest and that famous balance you're looking for between the exterior and the interior, between prayer and activity, between time for yourself and time for others. Everything will resolve itself through love. Stop wasting time running after the perfect community. Live your life fully in your community today. Stop seeing the flaws—and thank God there are some! Look rather at your own defects and know that you are forgiven and can, in your turn, forgive others and today enter into the conversion of love."

* * *

Sometimes it is easier to hear the cries of poor people who are far away than it is to hear the cries of your brothers and sisters in your community. There is nothing very splendid about responding to the cry of the person who is with you day after day and who gets on your nerves. Perhaps we can only respond to the cries of others when we have recognised and assumed the cry of our own wound.

* * *

Share your weakness

The other day, Colleen, who has been living in community for more than twenty-five years, told me: "I have always wanted to be transparent in community life. I have wanted more than anything to avoid being an obstacle to God's love for the others. Now I am beginning to discover that I am an obstacle and I always shall be. But isn't the recognition that I am an obstacle, sharing that with my brothers and sisters and asking their forgiveness, what community life is all about?" There is no ideal community. Any community is made up of people with all their richness, but also with their weakness and their poverty, of people who accept and forgive each other. Humility and trust are more at the foundation of community life than perfection and devotion.

* * *

To accept our weaknesses and those of others is the very opposite of sloppy complacency. It is not a fatalistic and hopeless acceptance. It is essentially a concern for truth, so that we do not live in illusion and can grow from where we are and not where we want to be, or where others want us to be. It is only when we are conscious of who we are and who the others are, with all our wealth and weakness, and when we are conscious of the call of God and the life He gives us, that we can build something together. The force for life should spring from the reality of who we are.

* * *

The more a community deepens, the weaker and the more sensitive its members become. You might think exactly the opposite—that as their trust in each other grows, they in fact grow stronger. So they do. But this doesn't dispel the fragility and sensitivity which are at the root of a new grace and which mean that people are becoming in some way dependent on each other. Love makes us weak and vulnerable, because it breaks down the barriers and protective armour we have built around ourselves. Love means letting others reach us and becoming sensitive enough to reach them. The cement of unity is interdependence.

* * *

Didier expressed this in his own way during a community meeting: "A community is built like a house, with all sorts of different materials. Cement holds the stones together. And cement is made of sand and lime, which are very insubstantial— it takes only a gust of wind to blow them away in a cloud of dust. The cement that unites us in our community is the part of us that is weakest and smallest."

* * *

Community is made of the gentle concern that people show each other every day. It is made of small gestures, of services and sacrifices which say "I love you" and "I'm happy to be with you." It is letting the other go in front of you, not trying to prove that you are right in a discussion; it is taking small burdens from the other.

* * *

If living in community means letting down the barriers which protect our vulnerability and recognising and welcoming our weakness, and so growing, then people who are separated from their community are bound to feel terribly vulnerable. Those who live all the time in the struggles of society have to build an armour around their vulnerability.

People who have spent a long time at l'Arche sometimes discover a whole lot of aggression in themselves when they return to their family, which they find very hard to bear. They had thought that this aggression no longer existed. So they begin to doubt their calling and who they really are. But the aggression is to be expected, because they have been stripped of much of their personal armour in community. But they cannot live so openly with people who do not respect their vulnerability. They have to defend themselves.

* * *

Community is a living body

St Paul talks about the church, the community of the faithful, as a body—the mystical body. Every community is a body and we all belong to each other. This feeling of belonging comes not from flesh and blood, but from a call from God. Each of us has been personally called to live together, to belong to the same community, the same body. This call is the foundation of our decision to commit ourselves with others and for others, responsible for each other.

> "For as in one body we have many members, and all the members do not have the same function, so we, though many, are one body in Christ, and individually members one of another."
>
> (Romans 12,4-5)

In this body, each member has a role to play: "the foot needs the hand", says St Paul; hearing and sight complement the sense of smell . . .

> " . . . The parts of the body which seem to be weaker are indispensable . . . God has so adjusted the body, giving the greater honour to the inferior part, that there may be no discord in the body, but that the members may have the same care for one another. If one member suffers, all suffer together; if one member is honoured, all rejoice together."
>
> (1 Corinthians 12; 22,24-6)

And in this body, each member has a different gift to offer:

> " . . . according to the grace given to us . . . : if prophesy, in proportion to our faith; if service, in our serving; he who teaches, in his teaching; he who exhorts, in his exhortation; he who contributes, in liberality; he who gives aid, with zeal; he who does acts of mercy, with cheerfulness."
>
> (Romans 12,6-8)

This body which is community must act and give light for the work of love, the work of the Father. It must be a body that prays and a body which is merciful, so that it can cure and give life to those who are hopeless in their distress.

See too 1 Peter 4,10-11 and Ephesians 4,7-16.

* * *

Using our gifts

Using our gifts is building community. If we are not faithful to our gifts, we are harming the community and each of its members as well. So it is important that all members know what their gifts are, use them and take responsibility for developing them; it is important that the gift of each member is recognised and that each is accountable to the others for the use to which this gift is put. We all need each other's gifts, and so we have the right to know how they are used. We also have the duty to encourage their growth and fidelity to them. We will all find our place in community according to our gift. We will become not only useful but unique and necessary to the others. And so rivalry and jealousy will evaporate.

* * *

Elizabeth O'Connor's book, *The Eighth Day of Creation*,[1] gives some striking examples of St Paul's teaching. She tells the story of an old woman who joined the community. A group of people were discerning her gift with her. She believed she had none at all. The others were trying to comfort her: "Your gift is your presence." But that wasn't enough for her. Several months later she discovered what her gift was: it was to carry each member of the community by name before God in a prayer of intercession. When she shared her discovery with the others, she found her essential place in the community. The others knew that they somehow needed her and her prayer, if they were to exercise better their own gifts.

When I read that book, I realised how little we at l'Arche help each other to build community by sharing about our gifts. I realised how little sense we have of really depending on each other and how little we encourage each other to be faithful to our gifts.

* * *

Envy is one of the plagues that destroys community. It comes from people's ignorance of or lack of belief in their own gifts. If we were confident in our own gifts, we would not envy those of others.

* * *

Too many communities form—or deform—their members to make them all alike, as if this was a good quality, based on self-denial. These communities are founded on laws or rules. But it is the opposite which is important: we must all grow in our gift to build the community and make it more beautiful and more radiant, a clearer sign of the Kingdom.

We mustn't either look just at the obvious gift, the talent.

[1] Word Books Editor, Waco, Texas, 1971

There are hidden and latent gifts, much deeper ones, which are linked to the gifts of the Holy Spirit and to love. They too must flower.

* * *

Some people have outstanding talents. They are writers, artists, competent administrators. These talents can become gifts. But sometimes the individuals' personalities are so tied up in the activity that they exercise their talent chiefly for their own glory, or to prove themselves or to dominate. It is better then that these people do not exercise their talents in community, because they would find it too hard to use them for the good of others. What they have to discover is their deeper gift. Others, of course, are more open and flexible, or their personality is less formed and rigid. These people can use their abilities as a gift in the service of the community.

* * *

"In a Christian community, everything depends upon whether each individual is an indispensable link in a chain. Only when even the smallest link is securely interlocked is the chain unbreakable. A community which allows unemployed members to exist within it will perish because of them. It will be well, therefore, if every member receives a definite task to perform for the community, that he may know in hours of doubt that he, too, is not useless and unusable. Every Christian community must realise that not only do the weak need the strong, but also that the strong cannot exist without the weak. The elimination of the weak is the death of fellowship."[1]

* * *

Using our gift means building community. If we are not faithful, the edifice will be weakened. St Paul emphasises the importance of charismatic gifts in this building. But there are many others which are more directly linked to a quality of love. Bonhoeffer[2] speaks of the different ministries a community needs: holding one's tongue, humility, tenderness, silence in the face of criticism, listening, constant readiness to render small services, support of brothers, forgiveness, proclamation of the word, speaking truth and authority.

The gift is not necessarily linked to a function. It may be the

[1] Dietrich Bonhoeffer, *Living Together*, Harper & Row, New York, 1954
[2] ibid

quality of love which gives life to a function; it may be a quality of love which has nothing to do with any function. There are people who have the gift of being able to sense immediately, and even to live, the sufferings of others—that is the gift of compassion. There are others who know when something is going wrong and can pinpoint the cause—that is the gift of discernment. There are others who have the gift of light —they see clearly what is of fundamental concern to the community. Others have the gift of creating an atmosphere which brings joy, relaxation and individual growth. Others again have the gift of discerning what people need and supporting them. Others have the gift of welcome. Each person has a gift to use for the good and growth of all.

But in each person's heart of hearts there is also the deep and secret union with God, the Bridegroom, which corresponds to their secret and eternal name. We are certainly made to nurture others, each in our own way. But above all we are made to live this unique relationship with our Father and His son, Jesus. The gift is like the radiance of this secret union on the community. It flows from it and strengthens it.

* * *

Community is the place where we all feel free to be ourselves and have the confidence to say everything we live and think. Not all communities will get to this point, it's true. But this is the direction in which they should be going. As long as some people are afraid of expressing themselves, for fear of being judged or thought "idiotic", or of being rejected, there is still a long way to go. There should be a quality of listening at the heart of the community which tenderly respects everything that is most beautiful and true in the other.

Self-expression does not mean simply giving vent to all our frustrations and angers and what is going badly—though sometimes it is good to bring these out. It also means sharing our deep motivations and what we are living. It is often a way of using our gift to nurture others and help them grow.

* * *

The secret of the individual

Community is the place where each person grows towards interior freedom. It is the place where individual conscience,

23

union with God, awareness of love and capacity for gift and gratuity all grow. Community can never take precedence over individuals. In fact, its beauty and unity come from the radiance of each individual conscience, in its light, truth, love and free union with others.

Some communities—which are more groupings or sects—tend to suppress individual conscience in the interest of a greater unity. They tend to stop people from thinking, from having their own conscience. They tend to suppress whatever is secret and intimate in the individual, as if personal freedom cut across group unity and constituted treason. In this sort of place, everyone must think alike—so there is a manipulation of intelligence, a brainwashing. People become automatons. Unity here is based on fear—the fear of being yourself or of finding yourself alone if you leave the others, the fear of a tyrannical authority, the fear of occult forces and reprisals if you leave the group. Secret societies and sects have a very great attraction for people who lack self-confidence or have weak personalities, because they can feel more secure when they are totally linked to others, thinking what they think, obeying without question and being manipulated into a strong sense of solidarity. The individual submits to the power of the group, which it becomes almost impossible to leave. There is a sort of latent blackmail; individuals are compromised to the extent that they cannot leave.

In a true community, individuals are able to keep their own deepest secret, which need not be handed over to others, or even shared. There are some gifts of God, some sufferings and some sources of inspiration, which should not necessarily be given to the whole community. Individuals should be able to deepen their own personal conscience. It is exactly in this that the weakness and strength of the community lie. There is weakness because of the unknown of individual consciences; because they are free, people can deepen in gratuity and in the gift which helps build community, or can betray love, become more egotistical and so give up and harm the community. There is weakness too because if the individual union with God and the truth are paramount, people can, if God so calls them, find another place in the community and no longer assume the function that the community finds most useful;

they can even physically leave. The ways of God for the individual are not always those of either men or the people at the head of the community. But there is strength too in putting the individual first. There is nothing stronger than a heart which loves and is freely given to God and to others. Love is stronger than fear.

* * *

In his last talk with the apostles, Jesus prayed three times that they should be one as he and his Father were one, "that they should be consumed by unity." These words are sometimes applied to unity between Christians of different churches, but they apply first and above all to unity within communities. All communities should be working towards this unity: "one heart, one soul, one spirit."

It seems to me that we should ask a special gift of the Holy Spirit—the gift of unity in its deepest sense, and with all its implications. This is truly a gift of God to which we have the right and the duty to aspire.

This gift of community, of unity, will come only when all members of the community are truly themselves, living love totally and using their unique gifts. So the community becomes one, because it is fully under the influence of the Spirit.

Jesus's prayer is astonishing. His vision goes much further than our imagination or wishes. The union of the Father and the son is total. Each community should be working towards this union. But it can only reach it in and through the Holy Spirit. As long as we live, all we can do is to walk humbly towards it.

* * *

When two or three come together in his name, Jesus is there. Community is the sign of this presence; it is a sign of the church. Many people who believe in Jesus are living in some degree of distress—the battered wives, the people in mental hospitals, those who live alone because they are too fragile to live with others. All these people can put their trust in Jesus. Their suffering is a sign of his cross, a sign of a suffering church. But a community which prays and loves is a sign of the resurrection.

* * *

As long as there are fears and prejudices in the human heart, there will be war and bitter injustice. It is only when hearts are healed that the great political problems will be solved. Community is a place where people can be human beings, where they can be healed and strengthened in their deepest emotions, and where they can walk towards unity and interior freedom. As fears and prejudices diminish and trust in God and others grows, the community can radiate a witness to a style and quality of life which will bring a solution to the troubles of our world. The response to war is to live like brothers and sisters. The response to injustice is to share. The response to despair is a limitless trust and hope. The response to prejudice and hatred is forgiveness. To work for community is to work for humanity. To work for peace is to work for a true political solution; it is to work for the Kingdom of God. It is to work to enable every one to live and taste the secret joys of the human person united to the eternal.

* * *

2

COME INTO THE COVENANT

Recognising the bonds

Some people come into community because they are attracted
by a simple way of life, in which there is welcome and sharing
and where relationships come first. Sometimes too they are
afraid of the demands of life in "open" society. They hope to
find their growth in a life of spontaneity and celebration. But
they gradually discover that there is more to community life
than that. To remain faithful to it means accepting certain
disciplines and structures and daily making the effort to come
out of the shell of egoism. Then they discover that community
is not primarily a way of life—which is only a means to something else—but that they have been called by God to carry
others in their suffering and growth towards liberation, and to
be responsible for them. And that is demanding. It is not
simply a question either of becoming responsible for others
and being committed to them; it is also accepting to be carried
and loved by them, and to enter into a relationship of interdependence and into a covenant. And that is sometimes even
more difficult and demanding, because it implies a revelation
of one's own weakness.

This evolution towards a real responsibility for others is
sometimes blocked by fear. It is easier to stay on the level of a
pleasant way of life in which we keep our freedom and our
distance. But that means that we stop growing and shut ourselves up in our own small concerns and pleasures.

* * *

People enter community to be happy. They stay to make others happy.

* * *

Almost everyone finds their early days in a community ideal. It all seems perfect. They seem unable to see the drawbacks; they see only what is good. Everything is marvellous; everything is beautiful; they feel that they are surrounded by saints, heroes or at the least most exceptional people who are everything they want to be themselves.

And then comes the period of let-down—generally linked to a time of tiredness, a sense of loneliness or homesickness, some setback, a brush with authority. During this time of "depression", everything becomes dark; people no longer see anything but the faults of others and the community; everything gets on their nerves. They feel they are surrounded by hypocrites who either think only of rules, regulations and structures or who are completely disorganised and incompetent. Life becomes intolerable.

The greater their idealisation of the community at the start, the more they put the people at its head on pedestals, the greater the disenchantment. It's from a height that you fall down a precipice.

If people manage to get through this second period, they come to the third phase—that of realism and a true commitment, of *covenant*. Members of the community are no longer saints or devils, but people—each a mixture of good and bad, darkness and light, each growing and each with their own hope. It is at this time of realism that people put their roots down. The community is neither heaven nor hell, but planted firmly on earth, and they are ready to walk in it and with it. They accept the community and the other members as they are; they are confident that together they can grow towards something more beautiful.

Commitment in a community is not primarily something active, like joining a political party or trade union. Those need militants who give their time and energy and are ready to fight. A community is something quite different. It is the recognition by its members that they have been called by God to live together, love each other, pray and work together in response to the cry of the poor. And that comes first at the level

28

of being rather than of doing. Active commitment in a community is more or less preceded by a recognition that you are already "at home", that you are part of its body, that you have entered into a covenant with the others and with God and the poor who are waiting for the fruits of community. It is rather similar to marriage: couples recognise that something has been born between them and that they are made for each other, before they make the commitment. It is only when they have recognised this that they make the active decision to commit themselves to marriage and remain faithful to each other.

So in community everything starts with this recognition that you are made to be together. You wake up one morning knowing that the bonds have been woven; and then you make the active decision to commit yourself and promise faithfulness, which the community must confirm.

It's important not to let too much time pass between this recognition that the bonds or the covenant are there and the decision. That's the best way to miss the turning and end up in the ditch!

* * *

Henri Nouwen says that "true solitude far from being the opposite of community life is the place where we come to realise that we were together before we came together and that community life is not a creation of human will but an obedient response to the reality of our being united. Many people who have lived together for years and whose love for one another has been tested more than once know that the decisive experience in their life was not that they were able to hold together but that they were held together. That, in fact, we are a community not because we like each other or have a common task or project but because we are called together by God."[1]

* * *

You are responsible for your community

I went the other day to the solemn profession of the deaconess sisters of Rueil. The Mother Prioress put a cross round the neck of each sister who consecrated herself to God and said to her something which touched me:

[1] *Solitude and Community*, Worship, Jan. 1978

"Receive this cross. It is a sign that you belong to God at the heart of our community. From now on, this community is yours. And you are responsible, with us, for its fidelity."

Each person in a community is responsible for its fidelity— not just those at its head.

* * *

The sense of belonging to a people, the covenant, with the commitment that it implies, are at the heart of community life. But that leaves the question: Who are my people? Are my people simply those with whom I live and who have the same perspectives as I do, or are they those for whom the community has been created? Let me explain. Three people create community life in a slum, trying to live welcome and a quiet and loving presence. They came inspired by a universal love, the love of Jesus; they were sent, they want to witness to the love of God and proclaim the good news of the Gospel by their presence and their life. Are their people the group to which they belong, which sustains them spiritually and perhaps materially, or are they the people of the slum, the neighbours? For whom are they ready to give their lives?

The same question comes up at l'Arche. Is the community made up above all of assistants who freely choose to come, with roughly the same motivations, or is it above all the handicapped people who did not have this free choice but were placed? We do not want two communities—the helpers and the helped; we want one. That is the theory, but in practice there is a tendency for the assistants to make their own community and be satisfied with that. Truly to make community with the poorest and identify with them is harder and demands a certain death to self. The closer you are emotionally to the assistants, the less chance there is of being close to the poor. Your heart can't be everywhere at the same time.

This can be taken further. Should the community, "my people", be limited to those—both handicapped people and assistants—who live under the same roof? Doesn't it also include neighbours, people from the district, friends?

As people grow in love, as their hearts become more open and as a community in its narrow sense becomes mature, so does the reality of the community, of "my people", get larger.

But each person who lives in the community must still set their priorities. Where should they concentrate their energies? For whom will they give their life?

In the case of the three people living in the slum, shouldn't the group to which they belong become a root, which enables them to be closer to "their people" in the slum? Then there would be no conflict of influences or loyalty. Roots are there so that flowers and fruits can grow—and it's in the fruit that you find the seeds of tomorrow. In the same way, the unity between assistants at l'Arche is there to encourage them to become closer to the handicapped people and to create one community. Belonging in one sense doesn't rule out belonging in the other—they are there for each other. They are one because love is essentially gift, not possession.

* * *

Of course we enter community to live with others. But also and above all we come to live the goals of the community with them, to respond to a call from God, to respond to the cry of the poor. So the community becomes a true dwelling place where together we can grow to respond to the call.

* * *

A community is never there for itself. It belongs to something greater—to the poor, to humanity, to the church, to the universe. It is a gift, a witness to offer to all men. The community—those with whom we live—is only a starting point, to enable our hearts to open to this universal dimension. Community has no sense unless it is seen with its roots, its branches and its fruit.

* * *

Sometimes communities get a long way away from their goals. Their members do not know clearly who "their people" are; they don't know which cries they should respond to. They don't know why they should grow in light and peace and wholeness. They do not know that they are called to become a source of life for their suffering people.

* * *

Some people are afraid to go near those in distress; they don't want to risk being wounded in their hearts, because once wounded there is a bond, a covenant. So the poor person becomes a shepherd who leads them. In saying "yes" to the crucified of the world, you say "yes" to the Crucified One. And in saying "yes" to the Crucified One, you say "yes" to the crucified of the world. Jesus is hidden in the faces of the poor. The smallest gesture of love to the least significant of his brothers is a gesture of love to him. Jesus is the starving, the parched, the prisoner, the stranger, the naked, the sick, the dying. Jesus is the oppressed, the poor. To live with Jesus is to live with the poor. To live with the poor is to live with Jesus.

* * *

I am struck by the number of people who want to create or enter community. Their energies are so taken up by this aim that they no longer see reality or those beside them who need their attention and their touch. So their project blinds them. The best way to come into community is to have no project, but to live intensely, with all that means by way of work, openness to others, listening and welcome. Then the passage to life in community comes quite naturally.

* * *

A community which has got too far from its goals closes in on itself. It no longer lives to respond to a call to go beyond itself. Then there will be tensions, until it either falls apart or refinds its calling.

* * *

When we enter community, we enter into covenant with our brothers and sisters who are members of that community, but also, and above all, with our people who cry out and suffer—the poor and oppressed who are waiting for the good news.

Jesus read this passage of Isaiah in the temple: "The spirit of the Lord is upon me, because he has appointed me to preach the good news to the poor. He has sent me to proclaim release to the captives and recovering of sight to the blind, to set at liberty those who are oppressed, to proclaim the acceptable year of the Lord." And he added: "Today this scripture has been fulfilled in your hearing" (Luke 4,18-21).

A community is there not only for the growth of its members, but for the growth of the people for whom it is destined. When we know our people, when we have recognised their sufferings and our own responsibility towards them, then we are able to go beyond ourselves.

* * *

When we know our people, we also realise that we need them, that they and we are interdependent. We are not better than they are—we are there together, for each other. We are united in the covenant which flows from the covenant between God and His people, God and the poorest.

* * *

To enter into a covenant is to discover that there are bonds between us and our God, that we are made to be His children and to live in His light. We are called to the divine wedding feast.

To enter into a covenant is also to enter the heart of God and discover that we are made for our brothers and sisters and especially for the poorest who are without hope. There are those who discover first the covenant with God, and then the covenant with their people. There are those who discover first the covenant with their people and then the source of this covenant in the heart of God.

* * *

Some people don't manage to commit themselves to those in distress because they are too blinded by their own tears; they do not hear the cry of the poor because they are deafened by the sound of their own desires, their own projects. We enter into a covenant with the poor when we make the effort to stop listening to ourselves and grieving about our own small sufferings and worries.

Sometimes too people don't want to recognise "their people" because that seems to bring terrible demands. It means becoming responsible for suffering and anguished people, responsible for responding to their cry and going beyond themselves for them. We have to grow in wisdom, in love and in humility to be better able to serve our people and use our gift more fully. We know then for whom we must give our life.

* * *

There is a mystery in the heart of the poor. Jesus says that everything we do for the hungry, the thirsty, the naked, the sick, the prisoner or the stranger, we do for him: "All that you do for the least of my brothers, you do for me." The poor, in their total insecurity, their anguish and their destitution, identify with Jesus. Hidden in their radical poverty, in their obvious wounds, is the mystery of the presence of God.

Of course people who have no security and are destitute need bread. But as well as the bread they need a presence, another human heart which says: "Take heart: you are important in my eyes and I love you; you have a value; there is hope." They need a presence which reveals God's mercy, the mercy of a God who is a father, who loves and gives life.

There is a covenant between Jesus and the poor. There is a great mystery there.

* * *

It is written:

> " ... the people of Israel groaned under their bondage, and cried out for help, and their cry under bondage came up to God. And God heard their groaning, and *God remembered his covenant* ... "
>
> (Exodus 2,23-24)

Then Yahweh reveals himself to Moses and says:

> "I have seen the affliction of my people who are in Egypt and have heard their cry because of their taskmasters; I know their sufferings and I have come down to deliver them out of the hand of the Egyptians, and to bring them up out of that land to a good and broad land, a land flowing with milk and honey."
>
> (Exodus 3,7-8)

This covenant between God and the poor remains.

* * *

Christian communities continue the work of Jesus. They are sent to be a presence to the poor who are living in darkness and despair. The people who come into these communities also respond to the call and the cry of the weak and oppressed. They enter into the covenant with Jesus and the poor. They meet Jesus in the poor.

* * *

Those who come close to the poor do so first of all in a generous desire to help them and bring them relief; they often feel like saviours and put themselves on a pedestal. But once in contact with the poor, once touching them, establishing a loving and trusting relationship with them, the mystery unveils itself. At the heart of the insecurity of the poor there is a presence of Jesus. And so they discover the sacrament of the poor and enter the mystery of compassion. The poor seem to break down the barriers of powerfulness, of wealth, of ability

34

and of pride; they pierce the armour the human heart builds to protect itself. The poor reveal Jesus Christ. They reveal to those who have come to "help" them their own poverty and vulnerability. The poor also reveal their "helpers'"capacity for love, the forces of love in their hearts. The poor man has a mysterious power: in his weakness he is able to open hardened hearts and reveal the sources of living water within them. It is the tiny hand of the fearless child which can slip through the bars of the prison of egoism. He is the one who can open the lock and set free. And God hides himself in the child.

The poor teach us how to live the gospel. That is why they are the treasures of the Church.

* * *

When I came to Trosly Breuil, that small village north of Paris, I welcomed Raphael and Philippe. I invited them to come and live with me because of Jesus and his Gospel. That is how l'Arche was founded. When I welcomed those two men from an asylum, I knew it was for life. It would have been impossible to create bonds with them and then send them back to a hospital, or anywhere else. My goal, in starting l'Arche, was to found a family, a community with and for those who are weak and poor because of a mental handicap and who feel alone and abandoned.

I have gradually discovered their gift. At the start, I could believe myself to be generous. But living with Raphael and his brothers and sisters, I began to realise my own limitations and mixed motives. To enter into relationship with them, I have had to discover that I too am poor. I have had somehow to stop having "projects" so that I could discover the child in myself—the child of God. So it was that I discovered the covenant which unites me to those who are weaker and poorer; and so it was that Jesus invited me to enter in some way into the covenant which he has established with the poor.

Those who came to help me, discovered, like me, the grace at the heart of the poor. We are now "a people," a large family, a community. And I cannot imagine the possibility of breaking the bonds of that covenant. That would be the greatest infidelity of all.

Through the years, I am discovering that there is no contradiction between my life with the poor and my life of prayer and union with God. Of course Jesus reveals himself to me in the Eucharist and I need to spend time with him in silent prayer. But he reveals himself too in this life with my brothers and sisters. My fidelity to Jesus is also realised in my fidelity to my brothers and sisters of l'Arche and especially the poorest. If I give retreats and take the role of director, it is because of this covenant, which is the basis of my life. The rest is only service.

I stand in wonder before those in the church who consecrate themselves to God in a life of prayer and adoration. Others have a mission to make themselves available to announce the good news or act mercifully in the name of the church. I sense that my own place in the church and in human society is to walk with the poor and weak, so that each of us develops and we sustain each other in fidelity to our own deepest growth, on our journey towards a greater internal freedom and sometimes external autonomy.

Our community cannot be a religious community, nor even a Christian one, in the sense that everyone in it is linked to a church and is a Christian. We do not welcome poor people because they are Christian; we welcome them because they are handicapped and in distress. And surely those who come to live with us of their own accord—first to help and then quite simply because they recognise the bonds that unite us—can say "yes" to the covenant even if they do not share the same faith in Jesus. I know that my own covenant with the poor is linked to my covenant with Jesus. It is Jesus who called me to them; it is entirely through a gift of the Holy Spirit that I have been able to respond to their cry of anguish. For others, this faith can be less explicit.

But we are all called to the same fidelity. I want to remain faithful to this covenant with my brothers and sisters of l'Arche. I want to live and die with them.

* * *

The first call—an experience of peace

When people start the journey towards wholeness, the pilgrimage to the promised land, there is a moment when their deepest being has been touched. They have had a fundamental experience, as if the stone of their egoism had been struck by Moses' staff and water had sprung from it, or as if the stone which was over the tomb had been lifted and the deep self had been able to emerge. It is an experience—and perhaps only a very faint one—of rebirth, of liberation, of wonder; it is a time of betrothal with the universe, with the light, with others and with God. It is an experience of life in which we realise that we are fundamentally one with the universe and with God, while at the same time entirely ourselves in the most alive, light-filled and profound sense. It is the discovery that we are a spring of eternal life.

This experience at the start of our pilgrimage is like a fore-taste of our end, like the kiss which is the foretaste of marriage. This is the call. It guides our steps in revealing our final destiny. There is nothing more deeply personal than this moment of wonder. But it happens very often in a given context. It may be a meeting with a poor person, whose call awakens a response in us; we discover that there is a living spring hidden deep within us. It may be a meeting with individuals in a community who become models for us. In watching them and listening to them, we discover what we want to be; they reflect our own deepest self and we are mysteriously attracted to them. Or again, the call maybe more secret, hidden in the depths of our heart, awakened perhaps by the Gospel or some other writing. It is hidden in the secret part of the individual. It makes us feel that we have glimpsed the promised land, found ourselves "at home", found "our place." The experience is often such as to take someone into a community or change the orientation of their life.

This experience can be like an explosion of life, a luminous moment, flooded with peace, tranquility and light. Or it can be more humble—a touch of peace, a feeling of wellbeing, of being in "one's place" and with people for whom one was made. The experience gives a new hope; it is possible to keep walking because we have glimpsed something beyond the material world and beyond human limitations. We have glimpsed the possibility of happiness. We have glimpsed "heaven."

The experience has opened our deepest being. Once into the community and on our journey, clouds can obscure the sun and that deepest self can seem to be shut away again. But nevertheless, the first experience stays hidden in the heart's memory. We know from then on that our deepest life is light and love and that we must go on walking through the desert and the night of faith because we have had, at one moment, the revelation of our vocation.

* * *

When someone arrives in a community and feels completely at home, in perfect harmony with the others and with the community itself, that is a sign that they are perhaps called to stay there. This feeling is often a call from God which must be confirmed by the call of the community. The covenant is the meeting of two calls which confirm each other.

* * *

When we are very deeply attracted by the people who live in a community it is a sign that perhaps we too are called to enter into the same sort of covenant. Artistotle says somewhere that if we want really to know someone, we should ask him who his friends are.

* * *

Many young people don't seem to realise the importance and the depth of this feeling of wellbeing when they meet a community which manifests a call of God.

Of course doubt can creep in after that first experience. Drawn by the seductions of the wealth and concerns of the world, by fear of criticism, by difficulties and persecution, we can turn away from that revelation of the light. We look for excuses: "I'm not yet ready; I have to travel, look around, experience the world; we'll see in a few years." But often we won't see; we will be caught up in other affairs, we will have found other friends to overcome the feeling of loneliness, we will no longer have the chance of living that fundamental experience of belonging to a community of hope. We will set off on another road and the meeting with God will perhaps be of another sort, at another moment.

* * *

Jesus looked at the young man and loved him. He said to him: "You lack one thing; go, sell what you have and give to the poor and you will have treasure in heaven; and come, follow me" (Mark 10, 21). But the young man didn't trust him; he was afraid because his security was in his wealth. And because he was very wealthy, he went sadly away.

The call is an invitation: "Come with me." It is an invitation not primarily to generosity, but to a meeting in love.

* * *

I am sometimes very sad when I feel that people don't take this fundamental experience of the call seriously enough. It is as if they were wasting a treasure. They are going to waste time and perhaps even turn completely away from the light. And yet the earth is ringing with the cry of despair, of the starving, of the parched, with Jesus's cry "I am thirsty." These people do not believe enough in either themselves or the call; they do not know that there is a spring in them waiting to be freed to irrigate our parched world. So many young people do not know the beauty of the life that is in them and can grow.

* * *

You are called to enter into a covenant with God and with your brothers and sisters, especially the poorest among them. You must not hold back.

> "I therefore . . . beg you to lead a life worthy of the calling to which you have been called, with all lowliness and meekness, with patience, forbearing one another in love, eager to maintain the unity of the spirit in the bond of peace. There is one body and one spirit, just as you were called to the one hope that belongs to your call, one Lord, one faith, one baptism, one God and Father of us all, who is above all and through all and in all."
>
> (Ephesians 4,1-6)

* * *

Leave your father, your mother, your culture

To enter into a new covenant and belong to a new people, a community with new values, we have to leave another people—those with whom we have lived—with other values and other norms: wealth, possessions, social prestige, revolution, drugs, delinquence, whatever. This passage from one people to another can be a very painful uprooting and usually takes a long time. Many do not achieve it, because they do not want to choose or to cut themselves off from their old life. They keep a foot in each camp and live a compromise, without finding their real identity. They remain alone.

To enter into covenant, to follow the call to live in a community, you have to be able to choose. The fundamental experience is a gift of God which sometimes comes as a surprise. But this experience is fragile, like a little seed planted in the ground. After the initial experience, you have to know how to take its consequences and eliminate certain values to adopt new ones. So, gradually, comes the orientation towards a positive and definitive choice for community.

* * *

Some people dare not make this passage because they are frightened of betraying their first people, of being unfaithful; they are afraid of their fathers and ancestors, because to leave them and their way of life seems like judging them. Jesus said: "Anyone who loves father, mother, brother or sister more than me cannot be my disciple." To enter a Christian community and universal love, we have to put Jesus and his Beatitudes above our own family and its customs. Sometimes, it's true, the father or the ancestors exercise such pressure, based on fear, that it seems impossible to cut away from them.

Some people are afraid of entering into covenant because they are afraid of losing their identity. They are afraid that they will disappear, lose their personality and interior wealth if they become part of a group and adopt the principles of community discernment. This fear is not entirely false. When we come into community we leave something of ourselves and the rougher elements of our personality behind. Sometimes aggression, which enriches an individual, gives way to a greater ability to listen; impatience gives way to patience. A new strength is born and new gifts appear. But community doesn't suppress people's identities—far from it. It confirms their deepest identity; it calls on the most personal of gifts, the ones that are linked to the energy of love.

* * *

There is often an act of faith at the basis of commitment to community—a belief that we will be reborn there. When we live alone or in our families, we build our identity on professional success, the way we use our leisure and the joy of family life. Work in community doesn't always—and certainly not straight away—bring the same satisfaction and sense of identity. So we feel we have lost a bit of ourselves. We can only accept this amputation if we are carried by the community and in prayer. We have to know how to wait patiently for the moment of rebirth. The grain of wheat must die before new life can appear. The road can be long and the nights dark; we have to wait for the dawn.

Entering into the covenant is abandoning ourselves trustingly to a new life which is already hidden in the deepest part of ourselves and which—if we give it earth, water and sun—will be reborn with a new strength. And the harvest will come.

* * *

I am sometimes astonished at the way in which parents worry when their son or daughter becomes an assistant at l'Arche. They come and ask me to persuade their children to "do something serious." These parents seem somehow completely bound up in the idea that a university degree or a good marriage brings security; then, it seems, their child will be "provided for." Life in community, especially with handicapped people, seems to them like an insecure folly. They tell themselves that it is an adolescent fancy, that this immaturity will pass.

It is through parents like these that we discover the conflict between the values of community life and those of modern society. Their pressure is sometimes such that their child doesn't dare continue on the community road. Are the parents afraid that their children will judge them? Whatever the reason, it makes me sad to see people who call themselves "good Christians" crushing the finest aspirations of their children in the sacrosanct name of security.

Perhaps too, parents find it hard to distinguish between a sect which will use psychological pressures to seduce their child and a Christian community which will set them free. They might be comforted if their child was in a well-known religious order.

* * *

Commitment

Some people flee from commitment because they are frightened that if they put down roots in one soil they will curtail their freedom and never be able to put down roots elsewhere.

41

It is true that if you marry one woman you give up millions of others—and that's a curtailment of freedom! But freedom doesn't grow in the abstract: it grows in a particular soil with particular people. Interior growth is only possible when we commit ourselves with and to others.

* * *

Some people are able to say that they are at l'Arche for life a few days after they arrive. They feel so at ease, so at home, that they are sure they have found their harbour. For others, it takes longer; they gradually discover that they are at home and that they have no need to seek further. The time it takes to give a definite "yes" is different for each person.

* * *

I am more and more struck by the suffering of young people. It doesn't surprise me that some of them find it enormously difficult to commit themselves. Many of them have had a more or less unhappy and unstable childhood. Many have had very precocious sexual experiences, which can make later commitment more difficult. And then there is today's tendency to question everything. People are quick to challenge authority and anyone who tells them what to think. At the same time, there is the feeling that our world is changing with a terrible speed; everything is on the move. Young people can commit themselves for today—but tomorrow? We have to be very patient with young people who may in many ways lack inner structure and be incapable of giving a definite "yes." Their world is almost too existentialist. But if they find someone who is faithful to them, they will gradually discover what fidelity means and will be able then to commit themselves.

* * *

We should always remember that there is a time for everything—a time to walk and run and a time to stand still, a time to discover and a time to choose, a time of adolescence and a time of maturity. We should never force a plant to grow more quickly than it does naturally—that hurts and destroys it. People can only put down roots in a community when that meets their deep and secret desire and their choice is free—because putting down roots, like any commitment, implies a certain death.

We can only welcome this death if there is a call of a new

life which yearns to grow. Putting down roots is the passage from adolescence to maturity. It is Easter—a death for a resurrection. And we can decide only when our interior growth has reached a certain point, when by the grace of God and with a feeling of being "at home", we can say "Yes", "Amen", "May it be according to your word" to the call of Christ and our brothers and sisters, to the covenant. Roger Schutz says somewhere that the "yes" to commitment is the pivot around which our life turns; it is the spring around which we dance. It is an important stage in our growth towards interior liberation.

* * *

If a community puts pressure on its members to decide before their time has come, this is because the community itself has not yet found its freedom. It is too insecure; it clings to people. Perhaps it has grown too quickly, forced by an expansionist pride. If our communities are born from the will of God, if it is the Holy Spirit who is at the origin of them, our Heavenly Father will send the people we need. A community has to learn how to be cheerful about letting people leave and how to trust that God will send other brothers and sisters. "Oh people of little faith! Seek first the Kingdom of God and all the rest will be given in superabundance."

* * *

Our world has more and more need of "intermediate communities"—places where people can stay and find a certain interior freedom before they make their decision. They either cannot stay in their family or don't want to; they are not satisfied with life alone in an apartment, hotel or hostel. They need somewhere where they can find their interior liberation through a network of relationships and friendships, where they can be truly themselves without trying or pretending to be anything other than they are. It is in these intermediate communities that they will be able to shed what is weighing them down and preventing them from discovering their deep selves. It is only when they have been exposed to the poor and to other values that they will be free to choose and construct a project which is truly their own, not that of their parents or the people around them, nor something set up in reaction to it, but one which is born of a real choice of life, in response to an aspiration or a call.

For a community to play this "intermediate" role, it must have a basis of people who are really rooted there. Many young people come to l'Arche having left school, university or a job which is no longer satisfying. They are seekers. After a few years they discover who they really are and what they really want. Then they can either go into a more specifically religious community, marry, go back to work or take up studies which now really interest them.

Others choose to stay. The community is no longer simply their place of healing, a place where they feel good and happy, but the place where they have decided to put down their roots because they have discovered the call of God and a whole sense to life in community with handicapped people. Their personal project melts into the community's project; they no longer feel challenged by other people's plans to leave the community for something else. They too have their personal project: to stay in the community.

* * *

I more and more realise how many people living in community are still very immature emotionally. Perhaps they lacked a warm emotional environment when they were young, above all, authentic and trusting relationships with their parents. So they are on an emotional quest, preoccupied by and dependent on their relationships with people of the opposite sex. These people need the community to grow towards a greater maturity; they need a secure nest, an emotionally warm environment where they can establish deep relationships without danger. They need older people who have time to listen to them.

* * *

One of the first roles of a community is to be a loving and secure place in which single people can find the emotional equilibrium that married people find "at home." The community is a home, a place where people live — not a work-place, an hotel or a lodging house. Those who have accepted celibacy in response to a call from Jesus and the poor need this warm environment so that they can live joyfully; they need a rhythm of life in which they can respond to the silent call of Jesus and be with their brothers and sisters peacefully. If we force them to be workers before being people who have a heart and an emotional life, they will either become hard, look for marriage at any price, or leave for a place where they can live their celibacy in truth and tenderness. A community must respect the heart and the emotional needs of people. It is a place of growth.

* * *

I sense that many people are afraid of committing themselves in community because they have not yet resolved this question of celibacy and marriage—and they could be right to be afraid, because their time has not yet come. As long as people are seeking marriage, or the question remains unresolved, they dare not put down roots in a community.

It is good that there are people in a community who have not yet resolved the question. But it is equally good and necessary that there are others who have resolved it. For some, settling the question will mean a decision to remain celibate for the rest of their lives in response to a call from Jesus and the poor. They will renounce the wealth of family life in the hope of a gift from God and in the desire to be more open to Jesus, the poor and the Gospel. That does not mean that they will not suffer by this, at least at certain moments; but they put their faith and their hope in the call to live with Jesus and in community with the poor.

For others, resolving the question means abandoning themselves to events and to God and above all giving priority to their faith in and commitment to God and to a way of life. They have accepted to live community life fully, to commit themselves to the poor, to put prayer at the heart of their life. If marriage comes, it will come only in this context, so that the couple, and then they and their children, can live these deep aspirations.

It is important that those who do not commit themselves, because they are still asking themselves about marriage and feel incomplete because they have not been uniquely chosen, are honest in their recognition that essentially they are waiting. Some people criticise the community, but their criticisms are only a way of saying: "I don't want to commit myself"—they are part of a defence system. It would be more honest to say: "The time hasn't come when I can commit myself because essentially I want to get married and I put that before my commitment to an ideal of community life." It is important that people can share at this level and discover the real reason why they do not feel comfortable in the community. Clearly it is their right not to feel comfortable if their time has not yet come. But it is important too that others who hear the call of God or of the poor without shelter, come into community to be there as a sign of the Kingdom, a sign that love is possible and that there is hope.

* * *

In many ways communities are like families. But there are clear distinctions. To start a family, two people must choose each other and promise fidelity. It is the fidelity and love of these two people which brings peace, health and growth to the children who are born of their love. When we come into community, we do not promise to be faithful to one person. The parental roles—those of the people at the head of the conmunity—change according to the constitution, and we do not commit ourselves to live always with the same people. Community implies family and family needs a larger community. But the two are very different.

When there are families in a community, their own dynamic and originality must be respected. They must be enabled to forge their unity. A couple is not the same as two single people living together; it is two people who have become one.

* * *

When I meet couples who want to come to l'Arche, I notice that sometimes the husband is enthusiastic and full of idealism, while the wife has more reservations. So I ask her if she too really wants to live at l'Arche. She replies that she loves her husband a great deal and is ready to do what he wants. That sort of situation is not good. For a couple to be able to commit themselves to community, both must really want it and neither must have any doubts. They must be very united and they must have been through the crises that a couple usually go through in the early years of their marriage. If they haven't done this by the time they come into community, they will be able to find any number of ways to avoid resolving these problems.

* * *

More and more familites are committing themselves to community life these days. They want to live with others, as far as they can, and share a certain sort of life. They want to live a covenant with the poor and with Jesus Christ.

It is a great richness to have married people at l'Arche. Most of them cannot live in a house with handicapped people, because they need their own place. In fact, a family is itself a community and must never be sacrificed to the larger community. But even though families cannot live all the time with handicapped people, their presence in the community is important. Their love, their emotional stability, their children bring so much to the weaker people—and to us all.

* * *

The birth of hope

A great hope is growing at this time. I meet more and more young people and young families in particular who are discovering that their working life is inhuman. They may be earning a great deal of money, but at the expense of their family life. They get in late at night, their weekends are often taken up with business meetings, their energies are used up by their working world. It is hard for them to find the interior tranquility they need to live family life. They realise that they are becoming hyperactive and that they are neglecting the deepest parts of themselves.

Some are caught up in the race for professional promotion; they are afraid to change gear because they may not find a decent job and they don't want to lose the material advantages they have. But others realise how serious their situation has become; their love for their family and their desire for God are greater than their desire for possessions and professional prestige. They are looking for a life which is more human and Christian. They dream of living in community.

But it would be useful if they looked more closely at their motives before committing themselves. Is it that they want to leave an inhuman job? Is it that they are looking for a warmer family life? Or are they really looking for community with all its demands? They would do well to start by taking a simpler job, which is less well paid but gives them more leisure, so that they can gradually discover where their heart is. Perhaps they could get more involved in their parish or neighbourhood.

Once they have found a new equilibrium in their life, they will be able to think of becoming an integral part of a community. Then it would no longer be a dream but the end of a natural journey.

* * *

A new hope is indeed being born today. Some people are dreaming of Christian civilisation as it used to be; they dream of chivalry; they sense that the power of egoism, hatred and violence is reaching everywhere. Others want to harness these forces of violence to break up the old world of private property and "bourgeois" wealth. And finally, some see in the cracks of our civilisation the seeds of a new world. Individualism and technology have gone too far; the illusion of a better world based on economics and technique are evaporating. Across these cracks, some human hearts are being reborn and discovering that there is a hope within, and not outside, them—a hope that they can today love and create community because they believe in Jesus Christ. A renaissance is coming. Soon there will be a multitude of communities founded on adoration and presence to the poor, linked to each other and to the great communities of the church, which are themselves being renewed and have already been journeying for years and sometimes centuries. A new church is indeed being born.

* * *

In our time, when there is so much infidelity, when there are so many broken marriages, so many disturbed relationships, so many children who are angry with their parents, so many people who have not been faithful to their vows, more and more communities need to be born as signs of fidelity. Communities of students or friends who come together for a time can be signs of hope. But the communities whose members live a covenant with God, among themselves and above all with the poor who surround them, or live with them, are more important still. They are becoming signs of the fidelity of God.

The Hebrew word *hesed* expresses two things: fidelity and tenderness. In our civilisation we can be tender but unfaithful, and faithful without tenderness. The love of God is both tenderness and fidelity. Our world is waiting for communities of tenderness and fidelity. They are coming.

* * *

48

Other paths

Some people find it hard to live with others. They need a lot of time to themselves, a great sense of freedom and above all, no tensions. They simply must not feel under pressure; if they do, they will become depressed or aggressive. These people are often very sensitive and delicate; they have almost too great a richness of heart. They could not cope with the difficulties of community life. They are called rather to live alone or with a few privileged friends. They must not be made to think that because community life is not for them they have no place, gift or vocation. Their gift is different. They are called to be witnesses to love in another way. And they find a certain community life with friends or groups, with whom they meet regularly.

* * *

"Many people seek fellowship because they are afraid to be alone. Because they cannot stand loneliness, they are driven to seek the company of other people. There are Christians, too, who cannot endure being alone, who have had some bad experiences with themselves, who hope they will gain some help in association with others. They are generally disappointed. Then they blame the fellowship for what is really their own fault. The Christian community is not a spiritual sanatorium. . . . Let him who cannot be alone beware of community. But the reverse is also true, let him who is not in community beware of being alone."[1]

* * *

Listening to Therese the other day during a retreat, I realised that the availability of some single people could be a mysterious commitment. She read this prayer which she had written:

> "We who are not committed to you, Jesus, in either a consacrated celibacy or marriage, we who are not committed to our brothers in a community, are coming to renew our covenant with you.
> "We are still on the road to which you have called us, but whose name you haven't given us; we are carrying the poverty of not knowing where you are leading us.

[1] Dietrich Bonhoeffer, *Living Together*, Harper & Row, New York, 1954

"On this road, there is the wound of not being chosen, not being loved, not being waited for, not being touched. There is the wound of not choosing, not loving, not waiting, not touching. We don't belong. Our house is not a home; we have nowhere to lay our head.

"Even though we become impatient and depressed when faced with the choice of others, unhappy when faced with their efficiency, we still say "yes" to our road. We believe that it is the road of our fertility, the road we must take to grow in you.

"Because our hearts are poor and empty, they are available. We make them a place of welcome for our brothers. Because our hearts are poor and empty, they are wounded. We let the cry of our thirst rise to you.

"And we thank you, Lord, for the road of fertility you have chosen for us."

* * *

People with problems

I am discovering more and more how many people on their own are deeply lonely. They bring certain emotional problems with them into community, together with what may look like a "bad character" and is often the result of suffering and lack of understanding. It is good that these people can come into a community which will be a place of support, opening and growth for them. But clearly they are going to suffer there and make others suffer too. Perhaps they need a community whose life is a little more structured, where there is not too much sharing, where there are not too many meetings, which could make them explode. They need solitude and work. It would be sad if communities accepted only perfectly balanced, flexible, open and available people. Those with difficulties also have the right to the possibility of community life. But not all communities can welcome them. We need communities with different structures, to welcome people with different needs.

* * *

Belonging to two communities

More and more people these days belong to two communities. This is particularly true of religious who have sometimes spent many years in their own community and then commit themselves in another. This "double belonging" can work very well. The first community is like the mother-community with which

50

they keep deep bonds, while they flourish in the new one. But there are dangers and risks too, particularly when people have left the mother-community feeling let down, angry or frustrated—even if they do not articulate these feelings—and are looking for a place where they can better live and express their ideal. These people will gradually take their distance from the mother-community, but often do not have the freedom of heart they need to commit themselves fully to their new community. Because they are afraid of being let down a second time, they don't let their hearts be too deeply touched. They keep part of their heart and their being for themselves so that they are not too vulnerable and won't suffer if things don't work out. Even in the best circumstances, there is a difficulty: when the heart is increasingly in the second community, people don't know what sort of bonds they should keep with the mother-community.

* * *

When people come into a community, they are usually in a state where you can ask anything at all of them. It is true that people coming into community have a child's grace. They have left their responsibilities and the landmarks which enable them to make judgements and have come into a new world. So we can expect them to be open to anything. It is like a new birth. This time of childhood, of naivete, openness and availability, will last for varying amounts of time. Sooner or later, people begin to make judgements and become defensive. The risk for people who leave one community to go into another is that they will arrive as adults and not as children. They will come to offer service. They already know what to do. I really wonder whether anyone can commit themselves in a community if they do not first live a period of childhood there.

* * *

3

GROWTH

A community grows like a child

Each of us is on a journey—the journey of life. Each of us is a pilgrim on this road. The period of human growth, from the time when we are infants in our mother's womb to the day of our death, is both very long and very short. And this growth is set between two frailties—the weakness of the tiny child and that of the person who is dying.

There is a waxing and then a waning in activity. The child and adolescent are travelling towards adult maturity; it takes many years for them to reach it and the independence and strength that it implies. Then come illness and weariness and we become more and more dependent, until that dependence is total and we are once again like a tiny child.

While there is a waxing and then a waning in action and efficiency, growth can be continual at the level of the heart and of wisdom. There are some precise stages in the growth of the heart. Tiny children live by love and presence—the time of childhood is a time of trust. Adolescents live by generosity, utopian ideals and hope. Adults become realistic, commit themselves and assume responsibilities; this is the time of fidelity. Finally, old people refind the time of confidence which is also wisdom. They cannot be very active, so they have time to observe, to contemplate and to forgive. They have a whole sense of the meaning of human life, of acceptance and of realism. They know that living has not just to do with action and running; they know that it is also to do with welcome and loving. They have somehow got past the stage of proving themselves through efficiency.

Between each of these stages, there are steps to be crossed. Each of these demands preparation and education and must bring some suffering. Human life is this journey, this growth towards a more realistic and true love; it is a journey towards wholeness. Tiny children are unified in their weakness and their relationship with their mother. But as they grow, divisions begin to appear between their emotional life and their relationships, between their will and their psychological makeup, between interiority and exteriority, between what they live and what they say, between their dreams and reality. As they grow towards independence, their fears about their weakness, vulnerability and limitations, about suffering and death, become more conscious, and so do the barriers they throw up around their vulnerability. The journey of each of us is a journey towards the integration of our deep self with our qualities and weakness, our riches and our poverty, our light and our darkness.

* * *

To grow is to emerge gradually from a land where our vision is limited, where we are seeking and governed by egotistical pleasure, by our sympathies and antipathies, to a land of unlimited horizons and universal love, where we will love all men and desire their happiness.

* * *

Just as there are steps to cross in human life, so are there steps in the life of communities. And crossing these also demands preparation, education and a degree of suffering.

There are the steps of foundation, and launching, and then there are the steps in daily life. There is the time of ageing, at which many people are taken up with the values of the past, of the time when they first came to the community. There is the time of fidelity. These steps are less clear than those of human life, but they are still there. There are different stages in the way authority is exercised, in the evolution of structures of decision-making. The community and those responsible for it have to be vigilant that these passages are well made.

Many tensions in community come from the fact that some

people refuse to grow; yet the growth of a community depends on the growth of each of its members. There are always people who resist change; they are refusing to evolve. In the same way, in human life, many refuse growth and the demands of a new stage: they want to remain children, or they remain adolescent, or they refuse to grow old.

Community is always in a state of growth.

* * *

It is no easier to live in community after twenty years than it was at the start. On the contrary, in fact. People are always a little naive when they enter community; they have many illusions and they also have the grace they need to pull them away from an individual and egotistical life. People who have been travelling for twenty years in community know that it isn't easy. They are very conscious of their own limitations and those of others. They know the full weight of their own egoism.

Life in community is a little bit like that journey in the desert towards the promised land, towards interior liberation. The Jewish people only started to murmur against God when they had crossed the Red Sea. Before that, they were caught up in the extraordinary, by the adventure, by the taste for risk; any burden at all seemed preferable to slavery. It was only later, when they had forgotten what it had been like to be oppressed by the Egyptians and when the extraordinary had given way to the ordinariness of everyday life, that they murmured against Moses and felt they had had enough.

It is easy to keep the flame of heroism burning at the foundation of a community. The dialectic with the environment stimulates generosity of heart; no one wants to be beaten. It is much harder when months and years have passed and people find themselves faced with their own limitations. Things from which we think we are detached come back to tempt us: comfort, the law of least effort, the need for security, the fear of being disturbed. And we no longer have the strength to resist. We have less strength to control our tongues and to forgive; the barriers come up again and we hide behind them.

Communities, it's said, start in mystery and end in bureaucracy. And that is not entirely unfair. The essence of the challenge to a growing community is to adapt its structures so that they go on enabling the growth of individuals and do not simply conserve a tradition, still less a form of authority and a prestige.

These days, we tend to set spirit and structures in opposition to each other. The challenge is to create structures which serve the spirit and which are themselves nourishing. There is a way of exercising authority, of discerning and even of running the finances which is in the spirit of the Gospel and the Beatitudes and so makes these tasks sources of life.

* * *

Community means communion of heart and spirit; it is a network of relationships. But this implies a response to the cry of our brothers and sisters, a sense of responsibility for them. And this is demanding and disturbing. That is why it is very easy to replace relationships and the demands they bring with laws, rules and administrative devices. It is easier to obey a law than to love—and more a part of human nature as well. This is why some communities are swallowed up by rules and administration instead of growing in gratuity, welcome and gift.

* * *

From heroism to dailiness

It is quite easy to found a community. There are always plenty of courageous people who want to be heroes, are ready to sleep on the ground, to work hard hours each day, to live in dilapidated houses. It's not hard to camp—anyone can rough it for a time. So the problem is not in getting the community started—there's always enough energy for take-off. The problem comes when we are in orbit and going round and round the same circuit. The problem is in living with brothers and sisters whom we have not chosen but who have been given to us, and in working ever more truthfully towards the goals of the community.

A community which is just an explosion of heroism is not a true community. True community implies a way of life, a way of living and seeing reality; it implies above all fidelity in the daily round. And this is made up of simple things—getting meals, using and washing the dishes and using them again, going to meetings—as well as gift, joy and celebration.

A community is only being created when its members accept that they are not going to achieve great things, that they are not going to be heroes, but simply live each day with new hope, like children, in wonderment as the sun rises and in thanksgiving as it sets. Community is only being created when they have recognised that the greatness of man is to accept his insignificance, his human condition and his earth, and to thank God for having put in a finite body the seeds of eternity which are visible in small and daily gestures of love and forgiveness. The beauty of man is in this fidelity to the wonder of each day.

* * *

Intellectual stocktaking

After the time of heroism and struggle, after the initial period of wonderment, there comes a time of intellectual stocktaking — of realisation of the community's identity and its place in society, the church and the very history of humanity. Vision and intellectual understanding are important to the life of a community. But intellectual consciousness must always spring from wonder and thanksgiving. If they are not at the heart of the community, it will age prematurely.

* * *

Marxist philosophers take the struggle against injustice and class warfare as their starting point, rather than an attitude of trust and wonder. That is why there are no Marxist communities, but only groupings of militants. If people come together just to fight, there is no love for or trust in the other; there is no thanksgiving.

A community must always remain a community of children — but children who are intellectually conscious and have a vision. A community which becomes a community of adults, of the "wise" and the "prudent", who see themselves as leaders of the struggle, very quickly loses its sense that it is a community at all. It becomes a group of hyperactive people who lose themselves in that struggle.

* * *

The Marxist critique of communities is sometimes hard to answer and many people succumb to it. They are frightened of being categorised as bourgeois, weak or afraid of confrontation. A community's vision is long-term. Its members believe in slow growth, while the Marxists want revolution, even though they do not always know what they want at the end of it.

Communities are trying to live now what Marxists want "come the revolution." You need courage to stand up to their criticisms. All of us have a secret desire to be seen as saints, heroes, martyrs. We are afraid to be children, to be ourselves.

* * *

The more a community grows and puts down roots, the more it must discover its own deep meaning and own philosophy of life. The more it lives authentic human relationships, and the more it becomes a place to live in rather than a gathering of "doers", the more it must find answers to the fundamental questions. It must give a sense to suffering and death, marriage, sexuality, the place of man and woman and authority. It must grow in its sense of God and of prayer and religion. It must have a philosophy about poverty and wealth, professionalism (or technique) and gratuity (or heart). It must understand hope and anguish, normality and abnormality, and the injustices of the world. And it must find symbols to express the meaning of these fundamental realities. We cannot grow together in community and deepen in our relationships without taking on these questions. The community must express its response to them through its own tradition. And we have gradually to become conscious of the significance of this tradition.

* * *

From monarchy to democracy

The more a community grows, the more attention must be paid to the evolution of its structures. At the start, there is generally a founder, who behaves like a monarch; he is the leader who decides everything. He is the person who has a vision of what the community should be, and he decides what happens in the light of this vision. As others join him and his project, and as life is born in the heart of the community, the leader must learn to dispossess himself of "his" project and become one among other members of the community. Structures should evolve towards a democracy in which the original leader, while keeping the vision, acts as coordinator.

If the leader does not encourage this move towards democracy—or rather towards true community discernment—there is a risk that he will stifle people's abilities. Then their capacities

57

for growth in responsibility and intelligence will remain dormant; they will remain unfulfilled for the rest of their lives.

Evolution of structures is possible because the community is becoming larger and its members are growing spiritually; they are deepening in their commitment and so able to assume increasing responsibility. At l'Arche, we work over our constitution[1] fairly regularly, and that seems worthwhile. My own fear is that some communities stifle their members because they do not know how to modify their structures to enable the essential of the community to be better lived.

* * *

It is important that people have their own projects and responsibilities which allow them to take initiatives. But it is important too that these projects are confirmed by the community, or that they spring from community discernment. Otherwise, they will go against the flow of the community; they will be the projects of individuals who either want to prove that they know better than the community or really want to leave it. People in community often believe that they know better than it does, or see themselves as "saviours." Community discernment implies that all members, or at least all those with responsibility, try together to discover its real projects and direction. The vital thing is that discernment is approached without passion, so that no one feels the need to convince others or to impose particular notions. If everyone listens to each other's ideas, the truth will gradually and calmly emerge. This can take a long time, but it is worth it, because once the decision has been made, each member of the community will have a personal commitment to the project.

* * *

Some communities have been founded by an individual who needs to be a leader, to prove something, to create "his" project. A founder will always need help to avoid this trap and to clarify his own motives. He should not be alone; it is better if a community is founded by two or three people who discern together and share responsibility from the start.

Otherwise, the founder is in danger of throwing himself

---

[1] The goal and spirit of l'Arche are specified in a charter; the constitution deals with the government of the community.

entirely into his own creation; he does everything and becomes possessive of his "child." He can't bear criticism and listens only to those who agree with him—and he can always find people like that. A community will suffocate if its founder stifles the people who have come to help its brothers and sisters or tends to mistrust them, deny them a share in responsibility or prevent them from taking initiatives.

If someone starts a community in the desire to prove something through his "child", there is an unhealthy pride in him, which has to die. A community is there for the people who live in it, not for its founder. Responsibility is a cross which the founder carries, but which must very quickly be shared so that all the members realise their own particular gift. If the founder doesn't learn to withdraw gradually, the community will either die or be obliged to reject him.

* * *

From time to time I meet people who want to create a community. After fourteen years' experience of community life, I wouldn't advise anyone to do so! (There are, of course, exceptions, founded on real signs from God.) I advise people instead to go and live in an existing community and then, when the moment is right, that community will send them to found another. If people are to create a community, they need a sense of belonging and a sense of having been sent. We need someone to confirm and support us, to direct and advise us. The first Christian communities were founded by people who were members of the community of apostles and who prayed at Pentecost with Mary the mother of Jesus. They were sent and confirmed by the college of apostles.

* * *

Openness to the neighbourhood and the world

Before starting a community, it is important to make contact with the village or the neighbourhood in which it is to be. Too many communities are born without these initial contacts, and if they welcome people who are handicapped or distressed, that can lead to catastrophe. The neighbours reject them. The community, far from being a sign of hope, becomes an abcess. If the founders had taken time to explain their project to the neighbours, they would have got a more understanding welcome. And if the community could have welcomed the handicapped people of the village, the community would have been completely integrated in it. Time spent over several months creating contacts and forming bonds of friendship with the neighbours, before the community even starts, is never time wasted.

* * *

For a community to become a sign, its neighbours must see it as bringing something positive to the neighbourhood or village. It is good to have someone who can help people who are old or ill; it is good for the community's house to be always open as a refuge for people who suffer and are in need.

* * *

The more a community deepens and grows, the more integrated it must be in the neighbourhood. When it begins, a community is contained within the four walls of its house. But gradually it opens to neighbours and friends. Some communities begin to panic when they feel that their neighbours are becoming committed to them; they are frightened of losing their identity, of losing control.

But isn't this what true expansion means? There are times when it is important to knock down the walls of a community. This demands that each person respect the others' commitment and that their rights and responsibilities are clearly explained. Each person must become responsible for the others in a specific way. Each must freely bring something to the others and true bonds must be woven. This is how a small community can gradually become the yeast in the dough, a place of unity for all and between all.

* * *

As a community takes root in a neighbourhood and begins to grow, and as its neighbours become involved in it, it will inevitably become aware of social injustices which oppress people and prevent their growth, especially if they belong to disadvantaged minorities. And so the community will begin to take political stands. It will seek to modify laws and struggle against injustice. Perhaps it will become unpopular with the government, and the opposition will try to entice it to join its own struggle. It is hard for a community in this position to find the middle road between the two extremes.

* * *

Margarita Moyano, who works with young people in Taizé and on evangelization programmes in Argentina, reminded us at l'Arche that a butterfly has to break the cocoon if it is to live, and that every child commits a violence when it is born. A new society cannot be brought to birth without some violence. But this violence must spring from, and reinforce, communion and trust.

* * *

A community gradually discovers as it grows that it is not there simply for itself. It belongs to humanity. It has received a gift which must bear fruit for all men. If it closes in on itself, it will suffocate. When it begins, a community is like a seed which must grow to become a tree which will give abundant fruit, in which all the birds of the air can come to make their nests. It must open its arms wide and hold out its hands to give freely what it has freely received.

A community must always remember that it is a sign and witness for all mankind. Its members must be faithful to each other if they are to grow. But they must also be faithful as a sign and source of hope for all mankind.

* * *

A community has to be apart from society and open to it at the same time. To the extent that its values are different from those of society, it must necessarily be apart from it. If it is too open, it will never keep and deepen its own values; it will have no identity or life of its own. But if it is too enclosed, it will not grow and it will not see the true values which exist in society and in others outside it. It will fall into a dialectic: "I'm right, the others are wrong." It will become incapable of seeing its own darkness and flaws. A community is called to grow gradually in relationship with others, with its neighbours; each will help the other to grow. It is not a question of one being right and the other wrong; they are there to help each other.

There was a time, it seems, when the religious orders were too shut in on themselves; they were suffocating. They recognised this, and have become open to society. But some, perhaps, have gone too fast. They discarded their traditional clothing so that they could be closer to people outside; but they threw off their traditions and the sense of their beginnings as well. They lost their identity; they lost community.

The time when a community feels it is dying is not the time to change externals, like the rule or the habit. If it does this, then there is nothing left to hold people together. This is the time for interior renewal, for a renewed trust in personal relationships and prayer; it is the time to stay close to the poor and those in distress.

* * *

Times of trial: a step towards growth

No community grows without times of trial and difficulty; times of poverty, persecution, tension and internal and external struggles; times which destroy its balance and reveal its weakness; times of difficulty which are inevitable when a new step has to be taken.

Creating a community means struggling against all sorts of things. But once the community is launched, energies seem to evaporate and people seek distractions; they compromise with other values. This can be very marked in a therapeutic community. At the start, it accepts people who are difficult or depressed, people who break windows. Then gradually everyone settles down and if "window-breakers" arrive, they are unacceptable. The energies which used to be there to tackle all sorts of problems and to assume difficult people have dissipated. A time comes when we feel too comfortable together, and that complacency signals a decline in the quality of unity. That is why times of trial are important for a community: they force us to refind the quality of unity and the energy to face difficulties; they force us to refind a sense of urgency.

* * *

A community which is growing rich and seeks only to defend its goods and its reputation is dying. It has ceased to grow in love. A community is alive when it is poor and its members feel they have to work together and remain united, if only to ensure that they can all eat tomorrow!

* * *

It is often when a community is on the verge of breaking up that people agree to talk to each other and look each other in the eye. This is because they realise that it is a question of life or death, that everything will collapse if they do not do something decisive and radically different. Often we have to come to the edge of the precipice before we reach the moment of truth and recognise our own poverty and need of each other, and cry to God for help.

But times of trial will only unite a community if there is a strong enough trust in it to assume them. If one member of the community is very seriously injured in an accident, small personal frictions and interests disappear. A shock like that deepens unity and brings us up against the essential. A new solidarity is born, which enables us better to bear trials and overcome them.

* * *

The times of trial which destroy a superficial security often free new energies which had until then been hidden. Hope is reborn from the wound.

* * *

Tensions

Communities need tensions if they are to grow and deepen. Tensions come from conflicts within each person—conflicts born of a refusal of personal and community growth, conflicts between individual egoisms, conflicts born of a diminishing gratuity, of differing temperaments and individual psychological difficulties. These are natural tensions. Anguish is the normal reaction to being brought up against our own limitations and darkness, to the discovery of our own deep wound. Tension is the normal reaction to responsibilities we find hard because they make us feel insecure. We all weep inside at the successive deaths of our own interests. It is normal for us to rebel, to be frightened and feel tense when we are faced with difficult people who are not yet free from their own fears and aggression. It is normal that our own reserves of gratuity run low from time to time, because we are tired or going through personal tensions or sufferings. There are a thousand reasons for tension.

And each of them brings the whole community, as well as each individual member of it, face to face with its own poverty, inability to cope, weariness, aggression and depression. These can be important times to realise that the treasure of the community is in danger. When everything is going well, when the community feels it is living success, its members tend to let

63

their energies dissipate, and to listen less carefully to each other. Tensions bring people back to the reality of their helplessness. They oblige them to spend enough time in prayer and dialogue, to work patiently to overcome the crisis and rediscover lost unity. They make them understand that the community is more than just a human reality, that it also needs the spirit of God if it is to live and deepen. Tensions often mark the necessary step towards a greater unity as well, by revealing flaws which demand re-evaluation, reorganisation and a greater humility. Sometimes the brutal explosion of one tension simply reveals another which is latent. It is only when tension comes to a head like a boil that we can try to treat the infection at its roots.

* * *

There is nothing more prejudicial to community life than to mask tensions and pretend they do not exist, or to hide them behind a polite facade and flee from reality and dialogue. A tension or difficulty can be the sign of the approach of a new grace of God. It can announce God's passage through the community.

* * *

Tensions and times of trial often come only when the community has lost its sense of the essential, its initial vision, or when it has been unfaithful to the call of Christ and the poor. These tensions, then, are a call to new fidelity. If the community is to refind peace, it must ask God's forgiveness and beg Him to give it new light and strength.

* * *

We must accept tensions as an everyday fact, while at the same time trying to resolve them in a search for deepening and for truth. And resolution does not mean hasty confrontation. It is not by making a tension explode in the presence of all the people concerned that we will resolve it. People are not necessarily helped to overcome their limitations, egoism, jealousy and inability to enter into dialogue simply by being made conscious of them. In fact, this can sometimes shut people off in an even greater anguish, close to despair.

People can generally only become conscious of their limitations if at the same time they are given the strength to overcome these by being helped to discover their own capacities for love, goodness and positive action, and to regain confidence in themselves and the Holy Spirit. People cannot accept their own evil if they do not at the same time feel loved, respected and trusted. They cannot overcome their egoism and fears if they have not been helped to discover that they are lovable. This is the role of the people with responsibility: to seize the beauty and value of people who are tense and aggressive and to help others in the community to do the same. Then those people, knowing that they are not rejected, but accepted and loved, will gradually be able to allow their positive energies to flourish in the service of others.

And when the fears diminish, when people begin to listen to each other without prejudice and rejection, and to understand why others act the way they do, the tensions disappear. It is a question of accepting others and loving them with all their egoism and aggression. This mutual acceptance, which can gradually become a true welcoming of the other, takes time and patience. It can involve very many meetings, which may be laborious, and sensitivity in dialogue, as well as silent, peaceful and tender acceptance.

Tensions should neither be hidden nor be brought prematurely to a head. They should be taken on with a great deal of sensitivity, trust and hope, knowing that there is bound to be suffering. They should be approached with deep understanding and patience, with neither panic nor naive optimism, but with a realism born of a willingness to listen and a desire for truth.

* * *

Tensions may arise from the fact that some people are too set in their opinions. With time, these people become more open and discover that reality has other dimensions. Their vision is modified and the tensions disappear. That is why we have to be patient with tensions and not always seek a speedy resolution. If we act too quickly, we may push people to exaggerate their position instead of becoming more flexible.

* * *

Other tensions in community come from the fact that it contains almost opposed values. The attempt to harmonise these is the genius of community. We want l'Arche to be a Christian community, but also to work within the structures demanded by the state. Some people live one set of values more strongly than the other, and that is good. But this can sometimes bring tensions between people. These tensions diminish as the community and its members become more mature and reach a certain wisdom.

* * *

Other tensions again come from the fact that the community is evolving and new gifts or realities are appearing, which will gradually demand a new balance or even an evolution in the community's structures. It is vital that we do not panic when faced by these tensions, which cannot always be verbalised. We have to know how to wait for the moment when these questions can be discussed in peace and truth.

* * *

Individual growth towards love and wisdom is slow. A community's growth is even slower. Members of a community have to be great friends of time. They have to learn that many things will resolve themselves if they are given enough time. It can be a great mistake to want, in the name of clarity and truth, to push things too quickly to a resolution. Some people enjoy confrontation and highlighting divisions. This is not always healthy. It is better to be a friend of time. But clearly too, people should not pretend that problems don't exist by refusing to listen to the rumblings of discontent; they must be aware of the tensions.

* * *

Many tensions arise from a refusal to accept that authority has its failings. We are all looking for the ideal mother or father and when we do not find them, we feel anguished. These are good tensions: each person must discover that the people who carry authority are also human beings who can make mistakes, without losing confidence in authority itself. Each person has to grow in maturity to find a true and free relationship with authority. And authority has to be ready to evolve and to be less afraid.

* * *

In many communities, there is someone who is more fragile or difficult than the others, who seems to catalyse all their aggression and become the butt of their blame, criticism and mockery. All members of a community, in some corner of themselves, feel frustrated and guilty. These feelings can very quickly be felt as a sort of anguish—a sense that we are not comfortable with ourselves. So we project our own limitations and cowardice onto someone weaker than ourselves. This "scapegoat" for personal and collective anguish can be found in many communities.

Once the aggression, bullying or rejection are unleashed, they are not easy to control. And yet, for the health of the community, they have to be deflected from their target, because no community can live while one of its members is being persecuted. So another person, either consciously, or unconsciously under the inspiration of the Spirit, must absorb the aggression. They may do it by playing the fool. Then the aggression is gradually transformed and the crackle of tension is dissipated in the light of laughter.

* * *

Sending people away

Some communities break up under the pressure of internal schism and disruption. It is striking how quickly, after a time of grace and unity, the first Christian communities became divided and partisan. Some, for instance, took Paul's side; others supported Apollos (I Corinthians 3).

St. John talks of these deep divisions in his first letter. There had been real splits in the community; some people left, refusing to be in communion with the others or to accept the doctrine of the apostles or, in particular, the authority of John (1 John 2,19).

Judas himself lived with the eleven and with Jesus, but his heart was full of malice and jealousy, and long before Satan led him to the final act of betrayal, his heart had become separated from the hearts of the others. Jesus had called him, but very quickly—and for reasons we do not know—he decided to take advantage of his position to further his own glory and personal plan. He did not want to serve Jesus with the other apostles; he wanted to use Jesus for his own ambitions.

At what moment should someone whose heart seems completely separated from the community's, who is sowing disruption and trying to use weaker people for personal and destructive ends, be sent away? These people, whose hearts are filled with jealousy, are often extremely intelligent, with a considerable ability to seize and exploit failings in legitimate authority or the community's life. So they can appear clairvoyant, to have an ability to redress injustice and save the situation. They have their attraction; the know how to create divisions, sow confusion and sap authority. It seems unthinkable to let them go on dividing the community, especially when all attempts at dialogue with them have failed. But to send them away, especially when they have been in the community for a long time, also seems unbearable.

Jesus is clear; "If your brother sins against you, go and tell him his fault, between you and him alone. If he listens to you, you have gained your brother. But if he does not listen, take one or two others along with you, that every word may be confirmed by two or three witnesses. If he refuses to listen to them, tell it to the church; and if he refuses to listen even to the church, let him be to you as a Gentile and a tax-collector" (Matt. 18,15-17).

Only the people with responsibility in the community and its long-term members can decide that someone must go. But in doing this, they too must recognise their share of guilt. Perhaps they did not dare to take the person in hand and set up a dialogue as soon as the first inkling of divisions appeared; perhaps they let the situation drag on, hoping naively that everything would sort itself out. Perhaps they even exploited the disruptive individual. But a belated recognition of its mistakes should not inhibit the community from acting firmly. If someone is causing scandal among the members of the community, they must be separated. Jesus says: " . . . Whosoever causes one of these little ones who believe in me to sin, it would be better for him to have a great millstone fastened round his neck and to be drowned in the depth of the sea. Woe to the world for temptations to sin! For it is necessary that temptations come, but woe to the man by whom the temptation comes! And if your hand or your foot causes you to sin, cut it off and throw it from you; it is better for you to enter life maimed or lame than with two hands or two feet to be thrown into the eternal fire " (Matt. 18,6-8).

But at the same time, authority must not be too quick to cry scandal and send people away simply because they dispute it.

It is often a refusal to listen to these first disagreements which throws up a barrier of pride. If the points had been heard, if the weaknesses and mistakes of the community had been admitted and if something had been done to try to set them right, perhaps the disputes would have disappeared, or have been converted into positive energy for reform.

A community should not send people away simply because they are disturbing or have a difficult character, or seem to be in the wrong place, or are challenging it. The only people who should be sent away are those who have already cut themselves off from the community in their own hearts, who pose a real threat of scandal by influencing others against legitimate authority and sapping confidence in it. These people divide the community and deflect it from its first goals.

In this difficult area of division and schism, there can be no rules except those of patience, vigilance and firmness, and of respect for the community's structures and insistence on dialogue. In fact, as long as people are integrated into a group and have no opportunity to spread discord, there is no reason to send them away. It is rather a question of carrying them, supporting them and helping them in whatever ways we can. All members of the community must be on their guard against sowing discord, whether consciously or unconsciously. All of them must constantly seek to be instruments of unity. That doesn't, of course, mean that they must always agree with the people at the head of the community. But they must confront them in truth. None of us who lives in community is free from a point of pride, born of bruised susceptibility, which can, if we are not careful, invade our whole being.

* * *

The outsider's eye

I more and more realise that no community, whether large or small, can cope on its own. Very often its members are not able to resolve their tensions. They need help to grasp the way the community is evolving and to find new structures for the different stages of its growth. Every community seems to need regular visits from a friendly outsider. It needs someone to whom all its members feel they can talk and above all someone who can counsel its leaders, so helping the community to

69

evolve and discover the message of God which is hidden in the tensions.

* * *

Yves Beriot, a French educator, was saying some time ago how important it is for people to visit communities and act as sponges which soak up the anguish. All communities feel far from their ideal, and more or less unable to cope with the violence and anguish of the people they welcome. We are all far from the ideal of the Gospel and this brings a latent anguish and guilt which sap our creative energies and can lead to sadness and despair.

* * *

Communities need a sympathetic outsider who encourages them, takes the heat out of things, listens and asks questions. Members of a community are often so taken up in the immediate that they lose sight of the whole. They need an outsider to ask them about their vision, their work with individuals, the ways in which they meet. I'm not talking about an expert, a specialist or psychologist, but about someone with common-sense, and an understanding of people and human relationships who loves the community's fundamental goals.

* * *

This outsider or "sponge" who absorbs the anguish must also help communities to evaluate themselves. Self-evaluation is not common in France; it is more accepted in the United States. From time to time, and very freely, we should all evaluate our community life, to see where we should be putting more effort, and sense if we are losing our creativity and falling into habit and routine. We have to evaluate our meetings to see if they are really nourishing and living, or whether they are simply a waste of time.

* * *

This outsider is also the community's memory bank. It is always important to have someone coming in who can ask "Do you remember?" and remind us of our origins, history and traditions, of joyful times as well as sad ones. If a community is to be able to make projects for the future, it must have assimilated its past and have a sense of its own tradition.

* * *

External authority

At the beginning of every community there is a founder who gives it its spirit and vision and takes on final responsibility. But as the community grows and takes root, it has to establish a charter which defines its fundamental goals and spirit, and a constitution which specifies how it is governed and covers such things as the structure of authority, who decides what, and how people are elected or appointed to positions of responsibility. A community also needs some external authority which will prevent those who carry responsibility in future from deviating from the spirit and becoming tyrants who create their own project.

This guarantor is necessary because human beings are weak and fallible and the forces of evil outside and even within a community are such that if there is no external authority, the community will sooner or later decline. External authority recognises the value, importance and deeply human or Christian inspiration of the community and is committed to helping it to stay faithful to its charter and spirit. This authority cannot repair the inadequacies of the community, nor can it bring back its spirit once this has begun to fade. But in moments of conflict especially, it can support and bolster the community or those of its members who seem best able to ensure that the spirit continues.

As it grows and develops, a community should clarify its position in relation to both church and state. In the end, it is one or the other which will be its guarantor.

Some l'Arche communities are directed by private, non-profit-making corporations recognised by the state. Their board of directors is made up of people who are competent in human affairs and support the charter of l'Arche. It is they who are the legal guarantors of the community and of its leader.

Other Christian communities are linked to a bishop. It is he who approves the community with its charter and constitution; he is its guarantor.

I am a bit concerned about communities without any traditions which refuse to accept external authority. They will not outlive their founder for long and, if there is no external control at all, the founder will be in danger of making some serious mistakes.

* * *

If a therapeutic community has a doctor or psychiatrist, he is guaranteed by the state which gave him his licence to practice, and he is a member of a professional group. In the same way, a Christian community is joined to the church by its priest or minister. He is its link not only with the actual hierarchy of the church, and particularly the bishop of the diocese, but also with the whole tradition of the church since its foundation by Jesus Christ. It is to the apostles and their successors that Jesus said: "Do this in memory of me." It is thus that all Christian communities are joined to a hierarchy, a tradition and a church which is the mystical body of Christ.

* * *

Growth in individuals and growth in community

Each member of a community who grows in love and wisdom helps the growth of the whole community. Each person who refuses to grow, or is afraid to go forward, inhibits the community's growth. All the members of a community are responsible for their own growth and that of the community as a whole.

* * *

Human growth is to do with integrating our capacity for action with our heart. Too often, action springs from fear of relationships, of our own vulnerability, or of love; it comes from fear of dependence, of sexuality itself and of our own deep and hidden self. Action is too often a flight or a desire to prove something.

When we are at peace, when we have assumed our own deep wounds and weakness, when we are in touch with our own heart and capacity for tenderness, then actions flows from our true selves.

* * *

I do not know if it is possible for anyone to grow without opening their heart to a witness to whom they have revealed the call of God for them and the small steps which He asks them to take. It is important from time to time to evaluate with this witness whether we are on the right road and, if not, how we are to refind our way.

But at the same time we are all afraid of opening up before a witness. We are frightened of revealing the most secret part of ourselves. It is easier and less dangerous to say a little to a number of people. Our greatest power is over our own secret. We are frightened to reveal ourselves to a witness who can strip us of this power. Of course it is essential to have a total trust in the witness. He too must know his place.

* * *

Some people come to our l'Arche communities to help handicapped people. That is good. Others come because they want to grow and sense that they need others to help, stimulate and encourage them; they see the community as the place of their growth and apprenticeship. That is better.

Those who come because they feel they have something to bring to the life of handicapped people often get a shock when they start to become conscious of their own weaknesses and limitations and those of the other assistants. It is always easier to accept the weakness of handicapped people—we are there precisely because we expect it—than our own weakness, which often takes us by surprise. We want to see only good qualities in ourselves and other assistants.

Growth begins when we start to accept our own weakness.

* * *

I sometimes tend to behave as if everyone could live in community and grow through their own efforts towards universal love. With age and experience of community life, perhaps too with a growing faith, I'm becoming conscious of the limitations and weaknesses of human energy, and the forces of egoism, fear, aggression and self-assertion which govern human life and make up all the barriers which exist between people. We can only emerge from behind these barriers if the Spirit of God touches us, opens the barriers and heals and saves us.

Jesus was sent by the Father not to judge us and even less to condemn us to the prisons, limitations and dark places of our beings, but to forgive and free us, by planting the seeds of the Spirit in us. To grow in love is to allow this spirit of Jesus to grow in us.

Growth takes on another dimension when we allow Jesus to penetrate us to give us new life and new energy.

* * *

The hope is not in our own efforts to love. It is not in psychoanalysis which tries to throw light on the knots and blocks of our life, nor in a more equitable reorganisation of the political and economic structures which must have their effects on our personal lives. All this is perhaps necessary. But true growth comes from God, when we cry to Him from the depths of the abyss to let His Spirit penetrate us. Growth in love is a growth in the Spirit. The stages through which we must pass to grow in love are the stages through which we must pass to become more totally united to God.

* * *

If we are to grow in love, the prisons of our egoism must be unlocked. This implies suffering, constant effort and repeated choices. To reach maturity in love, to carry the cross of responsibility, we have to get beyond the enthusiasms, the utopias and the naivetes of adolescence.

* * *

It seems to me more and more that growth in the Holy Spirit brings us from a state of dreaming—and often illusion—to a state of realism. Each of us has our own dreams and projects, which prevent us from seeing ourselves clearly and accepting ourselves and others as we are. Dreams throw up strong barriers. They hide the psychological, human and spiritual poverty which we find hard to bear in ourselves. And sometimes it is difficult to distinguish between the dream-aspiration that motivates and inspires our lives and the dream-barriers which are flight and illusion.

The work of Jesus and his Holy Spirit is to touch us more deeply than do our dreams. When we discover that God lives in us and carries us, our dreams can disappear without leaving us depressed. We are held by the gift of faith and hope, that fine thread which binds us to God.

* * *

People in community ask how they can know if they and it are growing. St Paul gives a clear indication in his Epistle to the Corinthians: love is not heroic or extraordinary acts; it is not speaking in tongues, prophesying, knowing all the mysteries and all of science, or even having extraordinary faith, giving all one's goods to the poor or being martyred. Love is being patient, rendering service, not being jealous or proud, not talking all the time about oneself and exaggerating one's own qualities. Love is doing nothing which bruises others; it is putting the interests of others above our own. It is not being irritable, bitter, aggressive or searching for the ill in others; it is not rejoicing in injustice but seeking the truth in all things.

And in his letter to Galatians, St Paul says that growth in love is growth in joy and patience, goodness, generosity, fidelity, tenderness and self-control. It is the opposite of all our tendencies to division—hatred, quarreling, jealousy, rage, disputes, dissension, schism, desire and of all those dark tendencies which lead us to fornication, impurity, debauchery, idolatry, witchcraft, orgies and gluttony.

Perhaps the essential quality for anyone who lives in community is patience: a recognition that we, others and the whole community, take time to grow. Nothing is achieved in a day. If we are to live in community, we have to be friends of time.

And the friend of time doesn't spend all day saying: "I haven't got time." He doesn't fight with time. He accepts it and cherishes it.

* * *

Disillusionments

Peter had four disillusionments when he was following Jesus.

I imagine he was disillusioned when Jesus called him: part of him must have regretted leaving his family and his trade. But his love for Jesus and his hope enabled him to get over this first disillusionment. Then he was disillusioned because Jesus was not altogether as he would have wanted him. He would have preferred a Jesus who was prophetic and messianic, who didn't insist on washing the disciples' feet, who didn't speak of dying. The greatest disillusionment was when Jesus became weak and died. Then, Peter denied him—and that was his disillusionment with himself.

These are the four great disillusionments of community life. The first—which is certainly the least hard—comes when we arrive. There are always parts of us which cling to the values we have left behind. The second is the discovery that the community is not as perfect as we had thought, that it has its weaknesses and flaws. The ideal and our illusions crumble: we are faced with reality. The third disillusionment is when we feel misunderstood and even rejected by the community, when, for example, we are not elected to a position of responsibility, or do not get a job we had hoped for. And the fourth disillusionment is the hardest: our disillusionment with ourselves, because of the anger and frustration that boils up in us.

If we are to become totally integrated into a community, we must know how to pass through these disillusionments. They are all new deepenings—passages towards internal freedom.

* * *

It is terrible to see enthusiastic young people, with a great ideal of sharing and community life, becoming disillusioned, wounded and cynical. After a few years, they can lose all taste for giving, and shut themselves off in political movements or the illusions of psychoanalysis. That doesn't mean that either politics or psychoanalysis are unimportant. But it is sad when people are totally shut up in them because they have been disappointed or have not accepted their own limitations. There are false prophets in communities who attract and stimulate the enthusiastic, but who through lack of wisdom or pride lead young people towards disappointment. The world of community is full of illusions. It is not always easy to distinguish what is true from what is false, or to sense if the good grain will flourish or be stifled by the weeds. Those who are thinking of founding communities should surround themselves with people who are wise and know how to discern. I ask forgiveness of all those who came to my own community or others of l'Arche, full of enthusiasm, and who felt deceived by our lack of openness, our blocks, our lack of truth and our pride.

* * *

Maturity

People who make the covenant and choose community life are in danger of losing within a few years the eye of the child and the openness of the adolescent. They are at risk of shutting themselves in on their own territory. They tend to want to possess their function and their community. How, once we are committed to community life, can we ensure that we never stop growing and loving? How can we ensure that we keep walking towards an ever greater human insecurity? Once we have taken root in the ground, we have to continue to grow and this means being pruned, cut back and sometimes even broken so that we can go on bearing fruit.

There can be a danger that we define ourselves entirely by community activity and the responsibilities this brings. We can become hyperactive and not know either how to stop or how to relax. By doing things for other people all the time, and devoting ourselves to them, we become more and more identified with our function and the privileges this brings; then we cling jealously to these. We have a terrible unconscious fear of letting go, because that implies dying and confrontation with the emptiness inside us. Those who carry heavy responsibilities in a community must look at their own interior life: are they blotting it out, or dispersing it in activity, or are they trying to nurture it? It is too easy to live on the perifery of ourselves, using our superficial energies instead of constantly working to deepen our interiority and our contact with the silent places at our heart where God lives.

The more we become people of action and responsibility in our community, the more we must become people of contemplation. If we do not nurture our deep emotional life in prayer hidden in God, if we do not spend time in silence and if we do not know how to take time to live from the presence and gentleness of our brothers and sisters, we risk we risk becoming embittered. It is only to the extent that we nurture our own hearts that we can keep interior freedom. People who are hyperactive, fleeing from their deep selves and their wound, become tyrannical and their exercise of responsibility becomes intolerable, creating nothing but conflict.

* * *

It the Spirit has called people to make the first passage from the discovery of new horizons (the time of adolescence) to determination and choice in a community, He will guide them in their journey towards maturity and wisdom and help them grow at all times. But if the first passage is made at high noon, under a shining sun, often surrounded by friends, the second—that of renunciation—is often made at night. We feel alone and we are afraid because we are entering a world of confusion.

We begin to doubt the commitment we made in the heat of the day. We seem deeply broken in some ways. But this suffering is not useless. Through the renunciation we can reach a new wisdom of love. Some people who hold responsibilities in communities find themselves entering this suffering and renunciation. They see signs that God is demanding the supreme sacrifice of them: that they leave the community they created, to live a new stage of their lives elsewhere. When they leave, their hearts are broken and they feel confused. But through this night, God is guiding them towards a new resurrection.

* * *

We all carry our own deep wound, which is the wound of our loneliness. We find it hard to be alone, and we try to flee from this in hyperactivity, through television and in a million other ways. Some people think their wound of loneliness will be healed if they come into community. But they will be disappointed. While they are young, they can hide their disappointment behind the dynamic of generosity; they can flee from the present by projecting themselves into the future, into a hope that things will be better tomorrow. But towards the age of forty, the future is past and there are no more great projects; the wound is still there and we can become depressed, especially as we are now carrying all the guilt and apathy of the past. Then we have to realise that this wound is inherent in the human condition and that what we have to do is walk with it instead of fleeing from it. We cannot accept it until we discover that we are loved by God just as we are, and that the Holy Spirit in a mysterious way is living at the centre of the wound.

At the end of a few years in community, people often go through a crisis which has to do with this feeling of loneliness. They have believed, more or less consciously, that the community would suffice them in every way. But their wound remains and they feel deceived. And so they may turn to marriage in the hope that this will heal their wound. But there they are at risk of being disappointed again. People cannot really enter marriage unless they are trying to accept their wound and unless they are determined to live for the other.

* * *

Old Age

Old age is the most precious time of life, the one nearest eternity. There are two ways of growing old. There are old people who are anxious and bitter, living in the past and illusion, who criticise everything that goes on around them. Young people are repulsed by them; they are shut away in their sadness and loneliness, shrivelled up in themselves. But there are also old people with a child's heart, who have used their freedom from function and responsibility to find a new youth. They have the wonder of a child, but the wisdom of maturity as well. They have integrated their years of function and so can live without being attached to power. Their freedom of heart and their acceptance of their limitations and weakness makes them people whose radiance illuminates the whole community. They are gentle and merciful, symbols of compassion and forgiveness. They become a community's hidden treasures, sources of unity and life.

The need for models

There is a lot of talk about "formation" in certain religious communities. I wonder whether they would not do better to talk more about "filiation." This is a time when there is a flood of information—by which I mean a sum of knowledge which is unstructured and dispersed. Formation implies a synthesis, based on clear principles. But some knowledge, at a spiritual level, can only be transmitted by filiation.

One of the best ways of learning to pot is to live and work for many years with a master potter. There are things that can only be learned in this way: his love for the clay and the product, his way of welcoming clients, thousands of small details which express his love of his craft. Being a good potter is not just a question of knowing the techniques; it also means living in a certain spirit, in relationship with the universe and with beauty.

Today, many ministers and priests are formed in universities or seminaries, by professional teachers. In India, if you want to become a guru, you live with a guru until he confirms you and sends you out to be a guru who forms disciples in his turn. These days, we tend to believe that everything can be learned from books. We forget that there is another way to learn: by living with a master.

The knowledge of how to live in community doesn't come from books—even this one! It comes from a certain spirit, engendered by the environment, perhaps by a father or mother figure in the community, and especially by older brothers and sisters. The parent figures will give life by sowing hope in the heart. But then we need brothers and sisters with whom we can identify and who become our models.

* * *

We need models if we are to put down roots in community life and live the covenant that this implies. We need to live with people who are happy, who have already passed through certain stages and perhaps certain trials, and who have found an inner peace and a certain radiance. They don't give lessons; but we can enter into their radiance and want to become like them.

The eyes of young people in community are always fixed on their elders who have lived there for several years. If they appear sad and peevish, the young people will very quickly decide that they do not want to turn out like that; they will believe more or less explicitly that community makes people frustrated. If they see people who are united, relaxed and unafraid, they will take them as their references.

* * *

Prayer, service and community life

A growing community must integrate three elements: a life of silent prayer, a life of service and above all of listening to the poor, and a community life through which all its members can grow in their own gift. It is by looking at these three elements that a community can evaluate whether it is alive or not.

* * *

Some communities start by serving the poor. When they begin, their members are full of generosity—except towards the rich—and have a rather utopian ideal. Gradually, they discover the need for prayer and an inner life; they realise that their generosity is being burned up and that they are in danger of becoming a collection of hyper-actives who put all their energy into external things. For the sake of a social ideal, they are losing their inner life; they no longer know how to live. If they go on like this, they will end up by putting their struggle—the struggle between classes, against the state and the wealthy—above everything. They will become a political movement with Marxist tendencies; they will no longer be a community.

Other communities start with prayer—like many of the communities of the charismatic renewal. But gradually they discover the need to serve the poor and to develop real commitment to them. Opening to God in adoration and opening to the poor in welcome and service are the two poles of a community's growth, and signs of its health. And the community itself must grow towards a stronger sense of its own identity, like a body in which every member can exercise its gift and be recognised for it.

* * *

From doing to listening

Communities which start by serving the poor must gradually discover the gifts that those poor people bring. The communities start in generosity; they must grow in the ability to listen. In the end, the most important thing is not to do things for people who are poor and in distress, but to help them to have confidence in themselves and discover their own gifts. It isn't a question of arriving in a slum with the money to build a dispensary and a school. It is more a question of spending time with the people who live in the slum to help them discover their own needs and them together building what they want. Perhaps these buildings won't be as beautiful. But they will be more used and loved, because they will belong to everyone and not just to a foreigner who means well. It will take a long time. But all service which is really human takes time.

* * *

Some communities grow by listening to their members' needs for formation and well-being. This growth is usually material: the communities go for the best and most comfortable buildings, where everyone has their own room. These communities will die fairly quickly.

Other communities will grow by listening to the cry of the

poor. Most of the time, this leads them to become poorer themselves, so that they can be closer to the poor people.

* * *

When a community lets itself be guided in its growth by the cry of the poor and their needs, it will walk in the desert and it will be insecure. But it is assured of the promised land, not the one of security, but the one of peace and love. And it will be a community which is always alive.

* * *

Signs of health in a community

When people refuse to come to meetings and there is no longer a place of dialogue, when they are afraid to say what they think and the group is dominated by a single strong personality who inhibits the others, when people flee into outside activities instead of taking part in community ones, then the community is in danger. It is no longer home for the people who live there, but an hotel.

When the members of a community are no longer happy to live, pray and work together, but are constantly looking for outside compensations, when they talk all the time about themselves and their problems instead of their ideal of life and their response to the cry of the poor, these are signs of death.

When a community is healthy, it acts like a magnet. Young people commit themselves; visitors are happy to come there. When a community starts to be frightened of welcoming visitors and new people, when it starts to lay down so many restrictions and ask for so many guarantees that practically no one qualifies to come, when it starts to reject its own weakest and most difficult members—the old and the sick—these are bad signs. Then it no longer a community. It is becoming an efficient place of work.

It's a bad sign too when a community tries to structure itself to ensure total security for the future, when it has a lot of money in the bank. Gradually, it will eliminate all possible risk. It will no longer need God's help. It will cease to be poor.

The health of a community can be measured by the quality of its welcome of the unexpected visitor or someone who is poor, by the joy and simplicity of relationships between its members, by its creativity in response to the cry of the poor.

But it is measured above all by the ardour for and fidelity to its own essential goals: its presence to God and the poor.

It is important that communities discover the signs of disruption and deepening. From time to time they should set themselves to find out where they are. It is not always easy, for they have to learn to go through times of trial. But there are signs of life and death which should be discerned.

* * *

Openness to others

When a community is born, it is very difficult to know whether it is a real community or a sect. It is only by watching it grow over time that we can know the answer. A true community becomes more and more open; a sect seems open, but over time in fact becomes more and more closed. A sect is made up of people who believe that only they are right. They are incapable of listening; they are enclosed and fanatical; they find no truth outside themselves. Their members have lost their capacity for individual reflection; only they are elect, saved and perfect; everyone else is wrong. And in spite of the apparent joy and relaxation, there is an impression that these are weak personalities who have been more or less manipulated and who are imprisoned in a false friendship from which they'd find it hard to escape.

The language of elitism smells bad! It is not healthy to believe that we are the only ones to have captured truth and even less healthy to condemn others. These attitudes have nothing to do with the message of Jesus Christ. A Christian community is based on the recognition that we are all sinners and that we need to be forgiven each day and to forgive seventy times seven. "Judge not, and you will not be judged" (Luke 6,37). A Christian community should do as Jesus did: propose and not impose. Its attraction must lie in the radiance cast by the love of brothers.

Communities are also distinguished from sects by the fact that the members of a sect focus more and more on a single reference—their founder, prophet, shepherd, leader or saint. It is he who holds all the temporal and spiritual power and keeps all the members under control. They read only his writings and they live from his words alone. This false prophet refuses to

83

allow anyone but himself speak to the group; he dismisses anyone who could threaten his all-powerful authority. He surrounds himself with people who are weak, incapable of any personal thought.

At the start of a true community, the founder holds the spiritual and communal power; he is the reference for all decisions. But he must gradually help people to make contact with other references and journey towards their own inner freedom, so that they think freely, while remaining in the spirit of the community.

True Christian communities always have a multiplicity of references, from the founder, the Gospel, the whole tradition of the church, the bishop and the Holy Father (if they are Roman Catholic), to other Christians living in the spirit of Jesus. And then, most essentially, each member of the community must learn to take as their reference the spirit of Jesus living in themselves.

* * *

It is fairly natural and perhaps even necessary that a new community is taken up with its own originality and tends to idealise itself. It it didn't believe itself to be unique, perhaps it would never have been founded at all. It's like love, which always starts by idealisation of the other: a baby is always the most gorgeous in the world to its parents and a bride is always the most beautiful to her husband. With time, both parents and married couples become more realistic; perhaps too they become more committed, more faithful and more loving.

It is understandable that a new community should be turned in on itself, strongly conscious of its qualities and originality and giving thanks for these. At the start of a marriage, a couple has to take time to forge its unity, its own community. This isn't egoism, but a necessary stage in growth. With time, the community must stand back a little to discover the beauty and particular gifts of others, as well as its own limitations. Once it has found its own identity and discovered how the Holy Spirit is guiding it, it must be very attentive to the manifestations of the Spirit in others. It should not believe that it is the only community to have the privilege of being inspired by the Holy Spirit; it should listen to what the Spirit is saying to others. This will enable it to rediscover its own gifts and mission and encourage it to be more faithful to them. This in turn will enable it to discover its place in the church and in humanity as a whole. If it is not attentive, the community is at risk of missing a decisive turning point in its own growth.

*　*　*

One of the signs of life in a community is the creation of links with others. An inward-looking community will die of suffocation. Living communities are linked to others, making up a huge reservoir of love for the world. And as only one Spirit inspires and gives life, communities being born or reborn will be alike without ever even knowing each other; the seeds He sows across the world, like the prophetic seeds of tomorrow, have a common source. It is a sign of maturity for a community to bind itself in friendship with others; it knows its own identity, so doesn't need to make comparisons. It loves even the differences which distinguish it, because each community has its own gift which must flourish. These communities are complementary; they need each other. They are all branches of that unique community which is the church, the mystical body of Christ. He is the vine of which the communities are branches.

*　*　*

I am always amazed by the multiplicity of communities which exist, from those which go back to St Benedict and have been revitalised by love, to those which the Holy Spirit is bringing to birth today. Some are within the churches; others are outside any institution, bringing together young people with prophetic intuitions who are looking for a new way of life. All these communities are part of the vast invisible church. Each has its own spirit, way of life, rule and character. Each is unique.

There are communities founded on adoration and silent and contemplative prayer—the many Carmels, the Little Sisters of Bethlehem and all those monasteries whose communication is more non-verbal than verbal, living a tradition that goes back to St Bernard or St Theresa of Avila. Linked to these are the communities of the sisters of Dernstadt in Germany and of the Little Sisters and Little Brothers of Jesus, silent and prayerful, in slums and ghettos across the world, linking contemplation and a presence to the poor.

Then, there are all the communities of prayer which are linked to the charismatic renewal, in which people come together to pray while remaining very rooted in society. There are the "Foyers de Charité", welcoming retreatants across the world. Madonna House, founded by Catherine Doherty, is yet another example of Christian community based on prayer, manual work, announcing the Word and a very beautiful liturgy. There are ecumenical communities, like Taizé in France and Bundeena in Australia. There are communities which have as an immediate goal the welcome and care of the poorest people of all: the Brothers and Sisters Missionary of Charity, founded by Mother Theresa and Father Andrew in Calcutta. Some communities are more committed to social action. They aim to bring improvement to the life of oppressed and suffering people, like the communities of the Church of the Saviour in Washington, DC., The Catholic Worker communities, those of El Minuto de Dios in Colombia and Father Ted Kennedy's with the Aborigines in Sydney. And there are many others, which are in the world as signs of the Holy Spirit.

Personally, I am drawn by the communities whose roots are in the poorest neighbourhoods, or which welcome those who have been deeply wounded, like alcoholics, people coming out of prison, young people who are lost in drugs, delinquents or people with mental illnesses. There is not always much joy and fun in these communities, but there is great fidelity and acceptance of wounds. The faces of the people who work in them are lined with fatigue. They don't have time to come to community meetings; they seldom have beautiful liturgies or even celebrations; often, they can only come to snatches of the Mass because their work is so demanding. But in these communities we feel the presence of Jesus, who is close to the most rejected and wounded people of all.

* * *

As I think of all the communities throughout the world, struggling for growth, yearning to answer the call of Jesus and of the poor, I realise the need for a universal shepherd, a shepherd who yearns for unity, who has clarity of vision, who calls forth communities and who holds all people.

I am deeply touched by the election of John-Paul I and even more deeply touched by the election of John-Paul II.

How long will it take before people realise this deep need? How long will it take for catholics to understand the depths of their gift and to be confounded in humility? How long will it take catholics to recognize the beauty and gift in the protestant churches, especially their love of scripture and of announcing the Word? And one day will protestant churches discover the immensity of riches hidden in the Eucharist?

Yes, I yearn for this day.

* * *

Roger Schutz has a passion for unity and I would wish to have the same passion. In the Acts of the Council of Youth 1979 it is written:

> "A way exists to put an end to the scandal of the divisions among Christians and to allow the churches to join in a common creation: that every local community refer to a ministry of reconciliation at the heart of the People of God. These past few months, the eyes of many men and women have been opened more than ever before to the ministry of a universal pastor, 'attentive to serve humanity as such and not only catholics, to defend above all and in all places the rights of the human person and not only those of the church'(John XXIII)."

* * *

The focal point of fidelity

Communities are born, flourish and then often degenerate and die. You only have to look at the history of religious orders to see this: the enthusiasm, the ardour, the generosity of their beginnings disappears as they gradually become comfortable. They become mediocre and rules and law take precedence over spirit. There is nothing attractive about mediocre communities; they disappear.

It is important for communities to discover the focal point of fidelity which enables the spirit to stay strong, and what makes for deviation from it. There seem to me to be two essential— and linked—elements which lead to deviation: the search for security, or a weariness of insecurity, and a lack of fidelity to the initial vision which gave the foundation its spirit.

When a community is born, its founders have to struggle to survive and announce their ideal. So they find themselves confronted with contradictions and sometimes even persecution. These oblige the members of the community to emphasise their commitment; they strengthen motivation and encourage people to go beyond themselves to rely totally on Providence. Sometimes, only the direct intervention of God can save them. When they are stripped of all their wealth, of all security and human support, they must depend on God and the people around them to understand the witness of their life. They are obliged to remain faithful to prayer and the glow of their love; it is a question of life or death. Their total dependence guarantees their authenticity; their weakness is their strength.

But when a community has enough members to do all the work, when it has enough material goods, it can relax. It has strong structures. It is fairly secure. It's then that there is danger.

A French civil servant, working in social services, once said to me, after I had explained in detail what l'Arche was: "What you are up to is certainly very fine and I'm sure it is the ideal situation for handicapped people. But it depends completely on the motivation of the assistants. Does a government have the right to invest in a place which could disappear completely the day it can't find assistants who want to live that way? What guarantees can you give me?" Of course, I had none. But uncertainty about new assistants arriving and about how long those we have will stay is the insecurity of our community. People don't come because of the hours and conditions or pay we offer; they come because of the community's atmosphere. The day we look for material ways in which to guarantee enough assistants, is the day that l'Arche will die. It can be tiring and even agonising to live in insecurity. But insecurity is one of the only guarantees that a community will go on deepening and progressing and remain faithful.

* * *

Our focal point of fidelity at l'Arche is to live with handcapped people in the spirit of the Gospel and the Beatitudes. "To live with" is different from "to do for." It doesn't simply mean eating at the same table and sleeping under the same roof. It means that we create relationships of gratuity, truth and interdependence, that we listen to the handicapped people, that we recognise and marvel at their gifts. The day we become no more than professional workers and educational therapists is the day we stop being l'Arche—although of course "living with" does not exclude this professional aspect.

Other communities have a different focus of fidelity. For the sisters of Mother Theresa, it is to bring help to the most wounded and rejected people of all. For the Little Sisters of Foucauld, it is to live together in small groups, present to the poorest. For contemplative communities, it is to orientate the whole day to silent contemplation. For others, it is to live poverty. Each community must recognise its own focus of fidelity, its own essential vision. If it loses sight of this focal point, it will regress, because the essential has crumbled.

* * *

All members of the community have to be vigilant to remain insecure and so dependent on God, and to live in their own way the focal point of fidelity, the essential of the spirit. These two things have to be stressed. Otherwise, the community will fall into routine, doing things by the book. It will end up ossified.

At l'Arche, we have constantly to encourage each other in these two areas. All serious decisions must be seen in their light. Are we deciding this because we are afraid of insecurity? Does this decision reflect the essential of our life—our faith that Jesus is living in the poor and that we are called to live with them and receive from them?

* * *

There is always a prophetic element in the birth of a community. It is a new way of life, set up in reaction to other ways, or to fill a gap in society or the church. With time, this prophetic element tends to disappear and the community's members are in danger of looking not at the present, or to the future, but to the past, in an effort to maintain the spirit or tradition. But the prophetic spirit must always be there if the community is to remain alive and hopeful. There is a particular tension between the value of the past (spirit and tradition) the needs of the moment (a dialectic with society and its prevailing values) and the pull towards the future (prophecy).

The spirit of a community, in its essence, is not properly speaking a way of life. It is more than that: it is a hope, an incarnation of love. It is made concrete, though, in the way

authority is seen, in the sharing, obedience, poverty and creativity of communities and their members in the propagation of
life, or in the way they emphasise one activity rather than
another. The spirit, in effect, decides what is essential in their
life. It provides a scale of values.

But with time, this spirit may perhaps be dissipated, stifled
and obscured by routine or custom. The job of the responsible
people, and indeed all the members of the community, is to try
constantly to purify the spirit, clarify it and live it more truly.
It is in a way the gift of God to the family, the treasure which
He has entrusted to it in a special fashion; it must always be
there at the heart of the heart of the community. The community should always live in the spirit of its foundation. That
doesn't mean living as it did in its founder's time. But it does
mean having the same love, the same spirit and the same
courage.

* * *

The spirit and spirituality of a community are embodied in
particular traditions. It is important to respect these and explain their meaning and origin to new members, so that they
do not become routine but are constantly renewed and remain
alive.

There are traditions in the way the community lives important events like death, marriage and baptism, in the way birthdays are celebrated and new members welcomed. The songs
and actions around these events are not so important in themselves; but they affirm the fact that we are truly members of
the same family, with the same heart, soul and spirit. And they
have been passed down to us by those who came before us and
may now be with the Father. These traditions remind us that
the community didn't just happen, but was born at a specific
moment, that it has perhaps been through some hard times
and that what we are living today is the fruit of the work of
those who came before us.

It is always good for individuals, communities and indeed
nations to remember that their present situation is the result of
the thousands of gestures of love or hate that came before.
This obliges us to remember that the community of tomorrow
is being born of our fidelity to the present. We are all links in
the great chain of generations which makes up humanity. The

fact that our lives are not long in the sum of time gives us a true perspective on our community, and the place of each of us in it. We discover that we are at the same time very insignificant and very important, because each of our actions is preparing the humanity of tomorrow; it is a tiny contribution to the construction of the huge and glorious final humanity.

`   * * *

Generating life

A community cannot remain static. It is not an end in itself. It is like a fire which must spread even at the risk of burning out. A moment comes when a community can only grow through separation, sacrifice and gift. The more it finds unity, the more it must be prepared in some sense to lose it, through the free gift of some of its members who will create other networks of love and communities of peace.

That is the meaning of life. Life reproduces itself. Growth means the appearance of flowers and fruits, which carry the seeds of new life.

A community which jealously keeps its members to itself and doesn't take chances in this extraordinary work of procreation is running a far greater risk: the risk of withering away. If the corner isn't turned, if the evolution of a community towards greater gift is not encouraged, its members will become infantile, close to regression. They will become sterile and life will not flow through them. Like dead branches, they will be good only for the fire.

            * * *

So many communities are dead because the people who carry responsibility in them have not known how to encourage their young members to give life in the procreation of new communities. The time of love has passed and they have come to a stage of sterility and frustration. It will then be hard to refind the forces of love and life.

The moment when life is given is different for each kind and type of community and for each person. For some members, it means leaving for far-off places, with all the risks that this can bring. A community which has reached maturity is able to give a brother or sister to support another community in distress. For others, giving life means more truth and warmth in their welcome of the poor, the marginal person, the stranger. For others again, giving life means taking on the role of shepherd in the community by helping each member see the beauty of life and free themselves from egoism. For yet others, it is discovering and accepting their contemplative role in the community; it is carrying their brothers and sisters and the wounded and rejected of the world in their prayers, bringing them to life in a mysterious and hidden way. Whatever the expression, to give life is to enter into the mystery of the Father. It is to work with Him and become His instrument in the extraordinary work of procreation and liberation.

* * *

It is sometimes difficult for people who are responsible for distant communities to know what sort of bonds they should have with the community they came from and the people who hold responsibility there. The important thing is that the distant communities live deeply their own life and spirit and integrate with their own neighbourhood. Many members of missionary communities live a contradiction. They have come from a particular culture and they have brought their own customs and ways of living, eating, welcoming and celebrating to a foreign soil. The spirit they want to transmit is so much born of their own culture that in the end they transmit more of the culture than of the spirit. And their neighbours are lost. They are often either shocked or seduced by what is foreign to their own culture; they do not grasp the spirit. And those among them who want to commit themselves to the community are sometimes obliged to adopt customs which are foreign to their own mentality.

Too often, the anxiety for unity with the "mother-house", in a simply material way, takes precedence over the dynamic concern for love, the spirit and the goals of the community. Unity doesn't come by ensuring that everyone is living in exactly the same way across the world. It comes from a harmony of hearts in fidelity to the initial spirit of the community, with the grace of the Holy Spirit. Distant communities have to know how to die to some of the elements of their own culture so that they can better live the Beatitudes in their new one. They must have a great trust in God who has sent them so far to make a covenant with a new people.

The concern of the "mother-house" must be to help the new community put down roots and so become a source of life where it is. If the "mother-house" takes this attitude, it will quickly discover the grace of rejuvenation and openness which comes from a multiplicity of communities. The distant communities, which live in risk and difficulty, can become a source and hope for the "mother-house", which in turn can offer them the security they need to establish themselves in hard situations.

* * *

Expansion and taking root

The more a community grows and gives life, sometimes by sending some of its members far away, the deeper its roots must grow into its own soil. Expansion has to be accompanied by deepening. The more a tree grows, the stronger its roots must be; otherwise, it will be uprooted by the first storm. Jesus speaks of a house built on sand. A community's solid foundation is in the heart of God. It is God who is at the source of the community and the more it grows and expands, the more it needs people who stay close to this source.

* * *

There is external growth, which is nearly always in expansion. But there is also internal and secret growth. In monasteries and houses of prayer, this growth is a deeper rooting in prayer in Jesus. This is invisible, but it creates a tangible atmosphere: a lighter joy, a denser silence, a peace which touches people's hearts and leads some to a true experience of God.

* * *

Born from a wound

There is a mysterious link between suffering, offering and the gift of life—between sacrifice and expansion.

In one of our communities in India, a fairly severely handicapped man, who had only been with us for a short time, drowned in a well. An old friend of his father told us: "A just man must die if a work of God is to live."

I'm deeply convinced that people of action and of light can do nothing unless they rely on those who accept their suffering, immobility and prayer and offer these to make life possible. People who are old or sick and offer themselves to God can become the most precious members of a community—lightening conductors of grace. There is a mystery in the secret strength of those whose bodies are broken, who seem to do nothing all day, but who remain in the presence of God. Their immobility obliges them to keep their minds and hearts fixed on the essential, on the source of life itself. Their suffering and agony bears fruit; they give life.

> "Look at your own poverty
> welcome it
> cherish it
> don't be afraid
> share your death
> because thus you will share your love and your life."

* * *

Some communities are composed entirely of old people. Their time of expansion seems to be over and it is probably now too late for a young person to come into them. The gaiety and peace of these communities is sometimes astonishing. Their members know that their community is dying, but they don't mind. They want to live fully and to the end the grace they have been given. These communities have a lot to bring to our world: they teach us to accept setbacks and to die in peace. And it is their acceptance of their suffering and offering of their sacrifice that brings to birth new and dynamic communities.

In other communities, by contrast, old people are in terrible anguish in the face of their sterility. They have not discovered that this sterility can be transformed into a gift of life by offering and sacrifice.

* * *

From the wound at the heart of Christ on the cross came water and blood, the sign of the community of believers which is the church. Life sprang from this cross; death was transformed into resurrection. That is the mystery of life born from death.

* * *

The role of Providence

Before they enter community, people feel a call or attraction to a life oriented towards God and the values of love and justice, instead of towards the more egoistical and visible values of possession, comfort, prestige and power. This attraction can be very weak at first, but if we respond to it, it gradually grows and becomes incarnate in a true desire and deep need to give ourselves to God and to our brothers and sisters, especially the poorest among them. This call is already a certain experience of God.

With time and through contact with our brothers and sisters and mutual commitment, there is the discovery of Providence. God has called us not only as individuals, but with others. We have all heard and followed the same call. It is God who has brought us together and inspired us to love each other. It is He who is at the heart of community.

This experience of providence grows stronger with time, with the discovery that God has watched over the community in times of trial which could have destroyed it. Serious tensions have been resolved, people have arrived exactly when they were needed, there has been unexpected financial or material help, someone has found inner freedom and healing.

With time, the members of the community realise that God is close and is watching over them with love and tenderness. Then the experience of God is no longer personal but communal, and this generates peace and a luminous certainty. It enables the community to accept difficulties, times of trial, need or weakness with a new serenity. It even brings the courage the community needs to keep going through daily setbacks and sufferings, because it knows from experience that God is present and will answer its cry. But this recognition of the action of God in community life demands a very great fidelity.

Nor does the recognition lead to a sort of irresponsibility, a feeling that there is nothing to do because God will provide. Far from it. In fact, the recognition demands that a community cling to the essential of its vocation, whether this is prayer, welcoming the poor or openness to the Spirit. God will only watch over us if we try courageously to remain faithful and true in our search for the community's final goals and unity. And God only responds to our needs when we are working, sometimes very hard, to find true solutions. Sometimes He waits until we have exhausted our human resources before He answers our call.

* * *

The sin of becoming rich

At the start of a community, God's action can often be felt very tangibly; in the gift of a house or money, the arrival of the right person at the right time, or other external signs. Because of its poverty, the community is completely dependent on Him. It calls and He responds. It is faithful in prayer. It lives in insecurity, it welcomes whoever knocks on the door, it shares what it has with the poor, and tries to take all its decisions in the light of God. In these early days, it is often misunderstood by society: people judge it as utopian or quite simply crazy; to a degree, it is persecuted.

Then with time, people see that this crazy project is working; they discover its values and its radiance. The community is no longer persecuted; it is admired and becomes renowned. It has friends which meet its needs. Gradually, it becomes rich. It begins to make judgements. It becomes powerful.

Then there is danger. The community is no longer poor and humble; it is self-satisfied. It no longer turns to God as it did before; it no longer begs His help. Strong in its own experience, it knows how to go about things. It no longer takes decisions in the light of God; prayer becomes tepid. It closes its doors to the poor and the living God. It becomes proud. It needs to be jolted and to go through some serious trials if it is to refind its child-like quality and its dependence on God.

* * *

The prophet Ezekiel describes the Jewish community as a woman. When she was a child, struggling in her own blood, God rescued her, cared for her and saved her life. He took care of her. Then, at the time of love, He covered her with His shade; He made her beautiful and married her. She became a Queen. And by her union with her King and Bridegroom, she became powerful. Then she turned her eyes from her King; she looked at herself and believed she was the source of life. She found herself beautiful and looked for other lovers. She prostituted herself and was disgraced. But in the depths of her poverty and humiliation, God was waiting, faithful to His love. He took her back as in the time of her youth, because He is tender and good, slow to anger and full of mercy, because He is the God of forgiveness (Ezekiel, 16).

The first sin of a community is to turn its eyes from the one who called it to life, to look at itself instead. The second sin is to find itself beautiful and to believe itself to be a source of life. If it does this, it turns away from God and begins to compromise with society and the world; it becomes renowned. The third sin is that of despair. The community discovers that it is not a source of life, that it is poor, that it lacks vitality and creativity. And so it withdraws into its sadness, into the darkness of its poverty and death.

But God does not cease to wait, like the father of the prodigal son. Communities which have set aside the inspiration of God to rely on their own power should know how to return humbly to demand His forgiveness.

* * *

The risk of growth

When I started l'Arche, we were poor. I remember an old woman who came every Friday night to bring us soup, and others who brought us small gifts of food and money. Now, after fourteen years, when there is a house for sale in the village, its owners come first to see if we want it—at an inflated price, of course. We are known as the rich people of the village, even though our money comes from state subsidies. In the beginning, professional people ignored us. Now they come to visit us from miles around, even if they still find us a bit crazy. There were five or six of us in the first l'Arche house; now we are 350 in twenty-one different houses, not just at Trosly but scattered through neighbouring villages and the town of Compiegne.

Sometimes the assistants complain that l'Arche has become too big, that it is no longer possible to know each other well, as we used to. That is true; there is a danger in growth. But there is also a grace. And I have the feeling that we have followed the signs of Providence at the different stages of our growth. The danger is that we close in on our success, forgetting our first inspiration. The danger is that we become a professionally competent centre which has forgotten gratuity, that we put so much emphasis on structures and the rights of assistants that we forget that handicapped people need to be with brothers and sisters who give themselves to them and are committed to them. The danger is that we forget how to welcome and no longer see handicapped people as a gift of God.

* * *

Some communities should stay small, poor and prophetic, signs of the presence of God in a world which is becoming more and more materialistic. But other communities are called to grow. Their mission is to help not just a few privileged people but a growing number, to show that it is possible to keep a spirit alive in a large centre, to create structures which are sensitive to people and to exercise authority in a way that is both humane and Christian. The mission of the small, prophetic communities is to show a path. Larger communities must live the challenge of this path by creating structures which are just and good for a large number of people.

Personally, I'm happy that l'Arche in Trosly has grown. Each day brings the challenge of trying to live community with a large number of people, of creating structures which allow for the greatest possible participation and give each person the chance to take responsibility and initiatives, while maintaining a unity of spirit. I am happy that we have been able to welcome a large number of people who are wounded and in distress and that some sixty of them have been able, after a time with us, to find work and live independently, while keeping in touch with us.

The important thing is to remain open to the signs of Providence while growing, to go on listening to the cry and the needs of handicapped people who are at different stages of their lives, to continue to be welcoming, to be ready to found communities if there seems to be a need for them, and to accept new kinds of poverty each day—for material poverty is not the only one. The danger is that we close in on ourselves and our achievements. We have to pray that we keep going further along the road of insecurity.

One of the only things I regret about the growth of l'Arche is that we have not worked enough with the people of the village;

our growth has been rather at their expense and against their wishes. Now there is a good understanding with them. But there is still work to be done if l'Arche is to be integrated into the life of the village. It is important too, that all a community's growth doesn't happen in the same village or neighbourhood. That way, it could become overwhelming; it would also need structures which might turn out to be too heavy and centralised.

* * *

I was a stranger and you welcomed me

One of the risks that God will always ask of a community is that it welcomes visitors, especially the poorest people, the ones who disturb us. Very often God brings a particular message to the community through an unexpected guest, letter or telephone call. The day the community starts to turn away visitors and the unexpected, the day it calls a halt, is the day it is in danger of shutting itself off from the action of God. Staying open to Providence demands a very great availability. It has nothing to do with hiding behind structures, laws, traditions and what has worked in the past. It demands a quality of attentiveness from each member of the community and an awareness of daily reality with all its unexpected happenings and insecurity. We are too quick to want to defend our past traditions, and so to shut ourselves off from the new evolution that God wants of us. We want human security, not dependence on God.

This is why it is important that the members of the community remember together and with the new people who arrive, what Providence has done for them, and that they give thanks for it. The history of a community is important. It should be told and retold, written and repeated. We are so quick to forget what God has done! We have to remember time and again that God is at the origin of everything, and that it is He who has watched lovingly over the community. Thus it is that we refind the hope and the boldness we need to take new risks, and accept difficulties and suffering with courage and perseverance.

The whole of Holy Scripture, as the Jews recognise so well, is a constant reminder of how God has watched over His people. It is when we remember this that we find the confidence to continue without stumbling.

* * *

Be zealous and repent!

In the Book of Revelation, the Angel says to the church in Laodicea: "I know your works; you are neither cold nor hot. Would that you were cold or hot! So, because you are lukewarm, and neither cold nor hot, I will spew you out of my mouth. For you say, I am rich, I have prospered and I need nothing; not knowing that you are wretched, pitiable, poor, blind and naked. Therefore I counsel you to buy from me gold refined by fire that you may be rich (in faith) and white garments to clothe you (the clothing of the covenant) and to keep the shame of your nakedness from being seen, and salve to anoint your eyes, that you may see. Those whom I love, I reprove and chasten" (Revelation 3,15-19).

These words can be applied to many of our communities and to each of us, myself first of all.

> "Be zealous and repent! Behold, I stand at the door and knock; if anyone hears my voice and opens the door, I will come in to him and eat with him, and he with me."
>
> (Revelation 3,19-20)

It is sad to see communities which have let fall their first love (Revelation 2,4). We all need to be encouraged and stimulated to repent and set off again with a new enthusiasm and ardour. But for that, we have to reopen the doors of our hearts and let Jesus enter:

> "And I will betroth you to me for ever; I will betroth you to me in righteousness and in justice, in steadfast love and in mercy. I will betroth you to me in faithfulness, and you shall know the Lord."
>
> (Hosea 2,19-20)

* * *

When we are going through difficult times in community, there is a text of Isaiah which I find brings me support and light. The prophet is asking what fast will be pleasing to God — which has to do not with renouncing food, but with gestures of love towards the poor:

"to loose the bonds of injustice
to undo the thongs of the yoke
to let the oppressed go free
to share your bread with the hungry
to bring the homeless poor into your house
to cover the naked."

If we do that, we shall be luminous as the dawn; our deep wounds, the inner sores of sin, will be healed.

"Your righteousness shall go before you
and the glory of the Lord shall be your rear guard,
You will be enveloped in the protection of God.

And in the hard times
the Lord will respond when you call;
If you cry to Him from the depths of your poverty,
from your weakness and your weariness,
He will say Here I am
He will reveal Himself to you.

The Lord will guide you continually
He will nourish you in the desert,
He will give you water in arid places,
He will give you strength
He will make your bones strong."

(Isaiah 58,6-12)

And then, supported, guided, gathered in by the Lord, we shall be like irrigated gardens, full of flowers and life. We shall be like inexhaustable springs of water; we shall be able to spill over a parched humanity which is dying of thirst.

That is God's promise, if we give ourselves to the hungry, to those in distress and insecurity, to those who feel alone.

It is when we are close to the poor and defenceless—who need special protection for precisely that reason—that we are close to God.

When our communities become tepid, we should open our hearts and our doors to the poorest and respond faithfully to their cry.

Then God will always be there to sustain and guide us.

* * *

4

NOURISHMENT
GIVES US OUR DAILY BREAD

Growth need nourishment

Human beings need bread if they are to grow. If they don't
eat, they die. And if they are to grow spiritually, they, like
plants, need sun, water, air and soil. The soil is the community
—the place they are planted, take root, grow, give fruit and die
so that others may live.

In the parable of the sower, Jesus says that though we can
welcome the word of the Kingdom with joy, this word can be
stifled after a time by trials and difficulties, by worldly cares
and the attractions of wealth.

We human beings are made up of contradictions. Part of us
is attracted by the light and by God, and wants to care for our
brothers and sisters. Another part of us wants frivolity, possessions, domination or success; it wants to be surrounded by
approving friends, who will ward off sadness, depression or
aggression. We are so deeply divided that we will reflect
equally an environment which tends towards the light and concern for others and one which scorns these values and encourages the desire for power. As long as we are not clear in our
deep motivation and as long as we have not chosen our friends
and the place of our growth in its light, we will remain weak
and inconsistent, as changeable as weathercocks.

A community is the reflection of the people who make it up.
It has energy founded on hope, but it also has weariness, the
search for security and a fear of evolving to a greater maturity

of love and responsibility; it often reflects our fear of dying to our personal instincts.

To grow on the journey toward wholeness and a greater radiance of justice and truth, people, like a community itself, need real nourishment. Without it, the energies of hope will waste away; instead there will be a desire for pleasure and comfort, or a depressed weariness, or aggression, or a legalistic, bureaucratic approach.

* * *

Because of our individual richness and complexity, we all need different nourishments on this journey towards wholeness. Some of these feed our heart and ability to relate, some our intellect, others our capacity for generosity and action, others again our search for God and hunger for the infinite. People very often over-nourish one part of themselves and neglect others; then they grow without balance or unity.

In some communities, there are very generous and active people, who neglect the richness of their own hearts, the secret part of themselves; others listen well but need to feed their capacities for generosity and action; others again seek the presence of God in the secrecy of prayer but have to make an effort to hear the cries of their brothers and sisters.

The journey towards wholeness implies a deepening of personal life in peaceful encounter with God and others, while living community life fully and assuming responsibilities towards society, the church and the universe. This journey is a long one and we will need plenty of personal and communal nourishment during it—food for the heart, for the mind and for the spirit.

* * *

We are all in danger of living superficially, on the periphery of ourselves. We tend to react to immediate stimuli, to demands from individuals who confront us and to the need for "urgent" action; we tend to flee from the treasure hidden within us. When for one reason or another, we become aware of it, or when it is touched by an external event, we are nourished. We are nourished by everything that stirs the essential in us and brings it to consciousness. This may be a word, a reading, a meeting or a suffering: all these can reawaken our deepest heart and give hope.

* * *

Community life demands that we constantly go beyond our own resources. If we do not have the spiritual nourishment we need, we will close in on ourselves and on our own comfort and security, or throw ourselves into work as an escape. We will throw up walls around our sensitivity; we will perhaps be polite and obedient, but we will not love. And when you do not love, there is no hope and no joy. It is terrible to see people living sadly in community, without love. To live gratuitously, we have to be constantly nourished.

* * *

Food for each day

If we are to remain faithful to the daily round, we need daily manna. It may be ordinary, a bit tasteless. But it is the manna of fidelity to the covenant, to responsibility, to the small things of everyday life. It is the manna of meetings, of friendship, of looks and smiles that say "I love you" and warm the heart.

* * *

The essential nourishment is fidelity to the thousand and one small demands of each day, the effort to love and forgive "the enemy", and to welcome and accept community structures, with all this brings by way of cooperation with authority. It is fidelity in listening to the poor of the community, in accepting a simple and unheroic life. It is fidelity in directing personal projects towards the good of the community and its poorest members and in renouncing purely personal prestige.

This fidelity is based on the belief that it is Jesus who has called us to this covenant with the poor, our brothers and sisters. If he has chosen and called us, he will help us in the small things of everyday life. If we accept everyday responsibility, with a humble and trusting heart, he will accompany us and give us strength.

* * *

It is sad to see people forced to leave their community to find their nourishment elsewhere. Of course we all have to get away from time to time to rest and refind perspective. But it is essential for all of us to find the nourishment we need in daily life itself. If structures and meetings seem too heavy, and create tension and a sense of oppression, there is something wrong with either the community or the individual. Working structures and meetings should be nourishing. Sometimes organisation and structures are set against gratuity, just as professional competence is set against compassion, as if these values were incompatible. In community, we have to live structures in gratuity and use professional techniques with compassion.

* * *

If we are in community only to "do things", its daily life will not nourish us; we will be constantly thinking ahead, because we can always find something urgent to be done. If we live in a poor neighbourhood or with people in distress, we are constantly challenged. Daily life is only nourishing when we have discovered the wisdom of the present moment and the presence of God in small things. It is only nourishing when we have given up fighting reality and accept it, discovering the message and gift of the moment. If we see housework or cooking simply as chores which have to be got through, we will get tired and irritable; we will not be able to see the beauty around us. But if we discover that we live with God and our brothers and sisters through what has to be done in the present moment, we become peaceful. We stop looking to the future; we take time to live. We are no longer in a hurry because we have discovered that there is gift and grace in the present of the book-keeping, the meetings, the chores and the welcome.

* * *

Every day we ask Our Father to give us our daily bread. We are asking then for nourishment for our hearts, so that we will be alerted to the will of the Father and the needs of our brothers and sisters. Jesus said that his nourishment was to do his Father's will. And it's true that this communion with Our Father is the essential nourishment for living our daily life.

* * *

Times of wonder

Many people in community tend to see the times they are alone as times of revitalisation, as opposed to the times of "dedication" or "generosity" they spend with the community.

This means that they have not discovered the nourishment of community.

This comes in the moments when together we discover that we make up a single body, that we belong to each other and that God has called us to be together as a source of life for each other. These times of wonder become celebration. They are like a deep, peaceful and sometimes joyful realisation of our unity and call, of the essential of our lives and of the way that God is leading us. They are a gift, a message of God in the community which awakens the heart, stimulates the intelligence and gives back hope. We rejoice and give thanks that we are together; we become more conscious of God's love and call for the community.

These times of wonder come in our daily prayer together, at the Eucharist and in relaxation after meals. A community should be vigilant to welcome or encourage these times of grace. We have to seize the moment at each meeting to say the word which will create unity or make people relax and laugh, or bring us back to the essential.

These moments of wonder can come on all sorts of occasions —perhaps a deep warm silence after a brother or sister has shared his or her call, weakness or need for prayer; perhaps during a celebration when we are singing, playing and laughing together. So every community gathering must be carefully prepared, whether it is a liturgy, a meal, a weekend, a sharing or a Christmas or Easter celebration. Each of these can be occasions for wonder. When something unexpected happens during a celebration—as it often does—we become conscious of a moment of grace for the community, a passage of God, a deeper silence; our hearts are touched. We have to know how to make these moments last, savour them and let them deepen us and our unity.

I have noticed at l'Arche that the death of a brother or sister, or a serious accident, are very important moments for the community. They are times of grace and wonder, when we are all brought back to the essential, in deep silence.

* * *

Some time ago at l'Arche we set up *Agape*. Every two months, the people who have spent a year in the community and intend to stay on, whether they are labelled handicapped or not, meet together for three hours to celebrate, pray, eat and share together. It is a time when we can pray about the major concerns of the community, or share what is most important in our own lives. It is a time when everyone, and especially the handicapped people, can speak, and when we recognise that we all belong to each other.

* * *

Laughter is an important food. It is healing and nourishing for all the members of a community to burst out laughing until the tears run down their faces. We are not laughing at each other; we are laughing with each other.

* * *

Confirmation from outside

Those of us who live all the time in community are in danger of missing the special gift which God has given us; sometimes we can be blinkered by daily life. It is very easy to forget that the outside world has its problems too; we tend to see only our own troubles. So we need outsiders to tell us what is unique in our community and remind us of what is positive. Members of a community often need to be encouraged and confirmed, to hear that what they are doing is important for humanity and the church.

* * *

It is good that different types of Christian community meet to share their hope and their vision. It is good too that Christians meet to see how the Spirit is acting among them. It is encouraging and strengthening to discover the network of the Holy Spirit and the marvels of God across the world. We realise then that we are not alone with our problems and that there is a universal hope.

* * *

It is important to know what the Spirit is doing in the church, because He is always raising up providential men and women to show us the way. The most prophetic are sometimes the most deeply hidden during their lifetime. Few people knew Therese of Lisieux or Charles de Foucauld before their deaths.

* * *

The word as bread

Sharing the word can be a powerful means of piercing armours and routines to let the living waters flow. It can be a nourishment which brings strength, energy and a new hope. But only words that touch the heart can do this. It is they, not those which are abstract, based on research or reason, which reveal the faith, hope and love of the speaker. It is they which are like a heat-giving flame or water which brings life to parched earth. The logic and content of what is said is less important than the enthusiasm with which it is conveyed. The tone of voice shows whether the speaker wants to seem brilliant and knowledgeable, or whether he wants to nourish, to give freely and witness humbly to what has been given and freely received. The talks which nourish come from people who allow God to speak through their lips. These talks come from the deep, hidden and silent places where God lives, to nourish those same places in the listeners. The talk must come out of silence and peace and lead back to silence and peace. It makes the call come alive and it brings the listeners back to what is essential in the community.

* * *

Some people have the gift of speaking to the whole community, others to smaller groups. Those who feel incapable of speaking at all often believe that this demands great competence and a wealth of ideas. But people are touched by the simplest words—the ones that come with humility, truth and love. There is nothing in intellectually complex sermons to nourish hearts; they come from the head and are sterile. Members of a community need people who witness to the Gospel and what they live, and share their hope as well as their weakness and difficulties.

* * *

The word of God, of Jesus and of the Gospel are a bread of life of which we can never have enough. They touch the essential in us.

* * *

A community—and especially a Christian one—will always be running against the tide of society, with its individualistic values of wealth and comfort and resulting rejection of the people who get in the way of these. A Christian community constantly calls its members to share, welcome, become poorer and go beyond their own resources to a truer love.

So a Christian community will always be a stumbling block, a question mark and a source of unease for society. The people around it will very quickly feel challenged. So the community will either be rejected because it reveals the egoisms in people's hearts, or attractive because people sense in it a source of life and warmth. A Christian community will often be persecuted or rejected; people may try to belittle its ideal to make it less of a threat.

The great dangers of a community are the cares of the world and the attraction of wealth. We either get weary and look for comfort, or we become aggressive toward those who criticise and persecute us. Members of a community must always remember why they live as they do. They need to be reminded of the original call or challenge. If not, they will soon forget the meaning of the difficulties, poverty and purifications of community and begin to turn against them.

Communities always need warm and inspiring talks which remind them of these, bring back hope and strengthen their desire to walk against society's tide.

* * *

People need an intellectual understanding of the significance of their community. Individual and communal spirituality are not enough. They need a clear reminder of the meaning and place of the community in today's world and in the history of salvation. It is important too to be reminded of the precise goals of the community, its call and its origins. In too many communities, the essential is obscured in a thousand and one activities. Their members no longer know why they are together or to what they should be witnessing. They discuss the details but forget what brought them together.

* * *

Rest and relaxation

I often hear talk in our communities of directors or assistants who are "burned-out." These people have been too generous; they have thrown themselves into frenzied activity which has finally destroyed them emotionally. They have not known how to relax. People with responsibility must teach assistants the discipline of physical rest and relaxation—they must sometimes insist that they learn it. Assistants have to be shown how to find spiritual nourishment. And the responsible people must set an example.

Many people get burned out because this is what they want. Some part of them is rejecting the need to relax and find a harmonious rhythm of life for themselves. They are fleeing something in their over-activity. They may be too attached to their function, perhaps even identified with it. They have not yet learned how to live; they have not discovered the wisdom of the present moment.

These people need a shepherd who helps them look at themselves and discover what they are running away from. They need someone who helps them stand back and relax enough to clarify their own motives and become people living with other people, children among other children. God has given each of us an intelligence. It may not be very great, but it is great enough for us to reflect on what we need if we are to live what we are called to live—community. "Look into your hearts. What are you fleeing?"

* * *

These over-active people, it seems, can be fleeing from their own sensitivity. They may be afraid of their emotions, of their own sexuality. They need to reflect on their own deep needs and to refind the child in themselves which is crying because it feels alone. Our bodies need to relax, but so do our hearts, in secure and unthreatening relationships.

* * *

Many people are tense because they have not yet entered into the collective conscience of their community; they have not yet surrendered to its gift and call. They have not really made the passage from "the community for myself" to "myself for the community", perhaps because their fragility makes them want to prove something to themselves and others, or because, fundamentally, they have come to the community as a refuge. They will only relax when they have discovered their own gift and put it decisively at the community's service.

* * *

I once spent an evening with some Franciscans who share an apartment in the black quarter of Chicago. I very much liked their prior, who demanded a real discipline of the novices. They had to sleep for a certain number of hours a night and eat well. "If we do not care for our bodies, and if we do not find a rhythm of life we can sustain in the years to come", he said, "it is not worth us being here. Our job is to stay. It is too easy to come and live among the poor for the experience, to exploit them for our own spiritual ends and then to leave. What we have to do is stay."

* * *

Rest is one of the most important personal resources, and it has a whole discipline of its own. Sometimes, when we are over-tired, we tend to flit about, doing nothing and spending long hours talking into the night when we would do better to get more sleep. We all have to find our individual rhythm of relaxation and rest. A lot of aggression and disagreement has somatic causes. Some assistants in our communities would do well occasionally to take a long hot bath, go to bed and sleep for twelve or fourteen hours!

Before they come into community, many people live the sort of life which allows them to set their own pace of leisure and relaxation. When they arrive in community, they have to be constantly attentive to others. So it isn't surprising that after a time they become tired and even depressed. They will begin to wonder whether they are in the right place; they will sense a form of anger in themselves and often the least frustration becomes intolerable. This isn't surprising, either; they have not found their rhythm of relaxation in their new life; they are too strung up by their wish to do the right thing. When we come into community we have to take heed of these somatic changes. We have to be very patient with our bodies and know how to re-create ourselves and how to rest.

* * *

The more intense and difficult community life becomes, the more tensions and struggles it produces, the more we need times of relaxation. When we feel strung up, tense and incapable of praying or listening, then we should take some rest—or even get away for a few days.

Some people don't know what to do with free time. They spend hours just sitting about and talking. It is sad if people have no interest outside the community, if they have given up reading, if they don't enjoy simple pleasures like walking and listening to music. We have to help each other keep alive the personal interests which help us relax and re-create us.

* * *

It is always good to have a grandmother in the community who can remind its members that they have a body and emotions, that they often turn molehills into mountains and that they could do worse than to take a good rest!

* * *

It is easy to be generous for a few months or even years. But to be continually present to others and not only present but nourishing, to keep going in a fidelity which is reborn each morning, demands a discipline of body and spirit. We need a disciplined spiritual and intellectual nourishment.

* * *

Food for thought

It is important to feed the intelligence. It is important to understand nature and the wonders of the universe, and so reach a deeper understanding of the history of mankind and of salvation. All our minds are differently made; there are a thousand and one doors into the meaning of things and their mystery.

One of the dangers of our time is that information is reaching saturation point and we only register superficial knowledge. It is good to train our intelligence onto a tiny fragment of this huge body of knowledge which reflects the hugeness of the universe of things visible and invisible. If we look more deeply at a particular aspect—whether this is the growth cycle of the potato or the meaning of a single word of the Bible—we can touch the mystery through it. When we train our intelligence onto a single subject, we enter the world of wonder and contemplation. Our whole being is renewed when we touch the light of God hidden at the heart of things.

We don't read enough in our communities. Sometimes we hit on a book on psychology, and that is fine. But it could be more nourishing to read about nature and the mystery of death and resurrection which is enacted constantly all round us. We shouldn't read just what is useful; we should also try to understand for its own sake, because it is the gratuity of the light which is stimulating.

* * *

Growth as nourishment

One of the best resources is the feeling that we are growing and making progress. We can get discouraged if we think we are at a standstill. So often we need a shepherd or friend who will remind us that the growth is in fact happening. But we also have to be patient when we feel we aren't growing. We have to trust and remember that it was Jesus who brought us into the community. In winter, it seems that the trees aren't growing; they are waiting for the sun; they have to be pruned. So we need reminding too of the value of waiting and sacrifice.

* * *

I am personally helped a lot by seeing a handicapped person gradually coming out of anguish and spiritual death, by seeing the light come into their eyes and a smile to their lips—by seeing life rising in them. The rebirth of a human being makes all the weight of daily life in community seem worthwhile.

* * *

When I meet handicapped people who are dying of sorrow in the huge ward of a hospital, or who are aggressive and so shut away alone, I find the courage to continue and to create new communities which will welcome people with handicaps. These visits give me the nourishment I need to go on living with my brothers and sisters at l'Arche. When we understand the purpose and usefulness of a community, we find strength.

* * *

Dawn was explaining the other day that she found problems stimulating. "When everything is too easy, I close in on myself and my own concerns. When a handicapped person is calling out or there are problems in the community to which I must respond, I feel a strength growing in me. I need this stimulus."

* * *

The friend

A real friend, to whom we can say exactly what we feel, knowing that we will be listened to, encouraged and confirmed in love and tenderness, is an absolutely essential resource. When friendship encourages fidelity, it is the most beautiful thing of all. Aristotle calls it the flower of virtue; it has the gratuity of the flower. On the dark days, we need the refuge of friendship. When we feel flat or fed up, a letter from a friend can bring back peace and confidence. The Holy Spirit uses small things to comfort and strengthen us.

* * *

When some assistants at l'Arche are very tired, they need to talk and talk and talk. They need a friend who will listen to and take in a whole mass of words, sufferings and fears. They will only be at rest when they are freed of all this and the friend has accepted it.

* * *

All of us in community—and especially, perhaps, the people with responsibility—can carry a load of frustration which cannot always be expressed in a group without endangering the community itself. The more sensitive we are, the more we are weighed down by these feelings of frustration, anger, anxiety, incompetence, sadness and apathy. We have a tremendous need to pour all this out to someone in whom we feel secure. We may need to say how much we detest someone who challenges us, without being accused of a "lack of charity." We may need this outlet for our emotions if we are to refind peace. But the person who becomes our "dustbin" has to have the wisdom to collect all this without getting worked up about it, without trying to set everything right and without either judging or enjoying it; nor should they encourage bad feelings.

* * *

When we feel loved and appreciated for who we are, when we feel called by the poor, we are nourished in the depths of our hearts. And to be nourished by the love of others is a call to become a nourishment for those who suffer and are alone in distress. So we learn to become good for others. "We who are strong ought to bear with the failings of the weak, and not to please ourselves" (Romans 15,1). "Let no evil come out of your mouths, but only such as is good for edifying, as fits the occasion, that it may impart grace to those who hear" (Ephesians 4,29).

* * *

We should not be afraid of loving people and telling them that we love them. That is the greatest nourishment of all.

* * *

Sharing

Sometimes in our communities we share about why we came to l'Arche, and how, and about what seems vital to us. And in listening to each other, in discovering the routes we have taken, the ways in which God has led us and made us grow, we feel nourished. Hope is reborn of this sharing in community.

* * *

I am struck by how sharing our weakness and difficulties is more nourishing to others than sharing our qualities and successes. There is a fundamental tendency to become discouraged in community. We either believe that others are better than we are, or that they don't have to cope with the same problems. The discovery that we are all in the same boat and all have the same fears and weariness, can help us to continue. People are nourished by humility, because humility is truth, linked to a trust in God and in brothers and sisters. "I feel weak, but I trust you will give me strength."

* * *

One of the greatest sins of a community is perhaps a sort of sadness and moroseness. It is easy to spend our time with a few friends, criticising others, saying that we are fed up and that nothing is like it was in the good old days. This state of spirit, which you can read on people's faces, is a real cancer which can spread right through the body. Sadness, like love or joy, comes in waves which immediately spread. We are all responsible for the atmosphere of the community.

* * *

The eyes of the poor

Sometimes the greatest resource of all can be a small gesture of kindness from someone who is poor. It is often a gentle look from someone who is vulnerable which relaxes us, touches our heart and reminds us of what is essential. One day I went with some sisters of Mother Theresa to a slum in Bangalore where they looked after some people with leprosy. The sores stank and, humanly speaking, it was revolting. But the people there had light in their eyes. All I could do was hold the instruments the sisters were using, but I was glad to be there. The expressions and smiles of the people seemed to reach right into me and renew me. When I left, I felt an inexplicable joy, and it was they who had given it to me. I remember too an evening in a prison in Calgary, in Canada, where I spent three hours with the members of "Club 21"—the men who are serving more than twenty-one years for murder. They touched me and recharged my spirit. They changed something in me.

* * *

My heart is transformed by the smile of the poor person, the expression of the person in despair. They bring new energy flowing from me. They seem to break down barriers and so to bring me a new freedom.

It's the same with the smile of a child: even the hardest heart can't resist it. Contact with people who are weak is one of the most important nourishments in our lives. When we let ourselves be really touched by the gift of their presence, they leave something precious in our hearts.

If we remain at the level of "doing" something for people, we can stay behind our barriers of superiority. We have to welcome the gift of the poor with open hands. Jesus says: "What you do for the least significant of my brothers (the ones you don't notice and reject), you do for me." It's true.

We ask God each night in the l'Arche prayer to help us see in the sufferings of our wounded brothers and sisters the humble presence of the living Jesus.

* * *

The poor are always prophetic. As true prophets always point out, they reveal God's design. That is why we should take time to listen to them. And that means staying near them, because they speak quietly and infrequently; they are afraid to speak out, they lack confidence in themselves because they have been broken and oppressed. But if we listen to them, they will bring us back to the essential.

Father Arrupe, general of the Jesuits, said in a talk to American religious:[1]

"Effective solidarity of the religious with those who are truly

---

[1] *A New Service to the World of Today*, December 20, 1977

poor will be accompanied by solitude among the poor........
We will feel ourselves alone when we see that the labourer's
world does not understand our ideals, our motives and our
methods. In the depths of our soul we find ourselves in complete solitude. We need God and his power to be able to keep
working in the solitude of our solidarity... and, in the last
analysis, misunderstood and alone.

"This is why we see that many religious men and women
who are inserted into the world of the labourer have found a
new experience of God. In the experience of finding themselves alone and misunderstood, their soul is ripe for the ful-
ness of God. In this simple experience, they feel themselves
very small and yet open to value in a new way how God
speaks to them through those with whom they stand in solidarity. They see that those people, the marginal ones, even though
not often believers, have something divine to tell them through
thier suffering, their oppression, their abandonment.

"Here one understands true poverty; one rediscovers awareness of one's own incapacity and ignorance; one opens one's
soul to receive very profound instruction in the lives of the
poor, taught by God himself, by means of those rough faces,
these half-ruined lives. It is a new face of Christ discovered in
'the little ones'."

* * *

When I feel tired, I often go to La Forestière. This is a house
in my community which welcomes very handicapped people;
none of the nine who live there can talk, several can't walk and
in many ways they have only their heart and the emotional
relationships they express through their bodies. The assistants
who feed, bathe and care for them have to do this not at their
own rhythm, but at that of the handicapped people. Things
have to go at a pace which can welcome their least expression;
because they have no verbal skills, they have no way of enforc-
ing their views by raising their voice. So the assistants have to
be the more attentive to the many non-verbal communications,
and this adds greatly to their ability to welcome the whole
person. They become increasingly people of welcome and compassion. The slower rhythm and even the presence of the handicapped people makes me slow down, switch off my efficiency
motor, rest and recognise the presence of God. The poorest

117

people have an extraordinary power to heal the wounds in our
hearts. If we welcome them, they nourish us.

* * *

Personal prayer

When we live in community and everyday life is busy and
difficult, it is absolutely essential for us to have moments alone
to pray and meet God in silence and quietness. Otherwise, our
activity motor will become overheated and whizz around like a
chicken without a head.

The Little Sisters of Foucauld have a whole rhythm in their
rule of prayer and solitude: an hour a day, a half day a week,
a week a year and a year each 10 years. Interdependence grows
in community, but we have to avoid an unhealthy dependence.
We have to take time alone with Our Father, with Jesus.
Prayer is an attitude of trust in Our Father, seeking His will,
seeking to be a presence of love for brothers and sisters. Each
of us must know how to rest and unwind in silence and contemplation, heart to heart with God.

* * *

"Do not be afraid that your momentary withdrawal will be
detrimental to the community; and do not be afraid that an
increase in your personal love for God will in any way diminish your love for your neighbour. On the contrary, it will
enrich it."[1]

* * *

Sometimes when I am alone, a light is born within me. It is
like a wound of peace in which Jesus lives. And through this
wound, I can approach others without barriers, without the
fears and aggression I often feel, without everything that stands
in the way of dialogue, without the waves of egoism. So I can
remain in the presence of Jesus and the invisible presence of
my brothers and sisters. I discover more and more each day
my need for these times of solitude in which I can rediscover
others with more truth and accept, in the light of God, my own
weakness, ignorance, egoism and fear. This solitude does not
separate me from others; it helps me love them more tenderly,

[1] Carlo Caretto, *In Search of the Beyond*, Darton, Longman & Todd,
London, 1975.

118

realistically and attentively. I begin to distinguish too between the false solitude which is a flight from others to be alone with egoism, sadness or a bruised sensitivity, and the true solitude which is communion with God and others.

* * *

We all have to find our own rhythm of prayer. For some of us, this will mean praying for hours at a time, for others, for fifteen minutes here and there. For all of us, it is being attentive to God's presence and will throughout the day.

Some of us need the stimulus of the Word of God or saying the Our Father; others need to repeat the name of Jesus or Mary. Prayer is like a secret garden made up of silence and rest and inwardness. But there are a thousand and one doors into this garden and we all have to find our own.

If we do not pray, if we do not evaluate our activities and find rest in the secret part of our heart, it will be very hard to live in community. We will not be open to others, we will not be craftsmen of peace. We will live only from the stimuli of the present moment, and we will lose sight of our priorities and of the essential. We have to remember too that some purifications come only with the help of the Holy Spirit. Only God can shed light on some corners of our feelings and unconscious.

* * *

To pray is to surrender our whole being to God, letting Him take over the rudder of our existence. To pray is to trust, saying to God: "Here I am. Behold the handmaid of the Lord; may it be done unto me according to Thy word."

"We must learn to trust, refusing to set any value on what is felt, whether it be consolation or suffering."[1] We must learn to trust that God is calling us to grow in our community and calling our community to become a source in a parched world.

* * *

Prayer is a meeting which nourishes our hearts. It is presence and communion. The secret of our being is in this kiss of God by which we know we are loved and forgiven. In our deepest selves, below the levels of action and understanding, there is a

[1] Ruth Burrows, *Guidelines for Mystical Prayer*, Sheed and Ward, London, 1976. Her other books: *Before the Living God* and *To Believe in Jesus* are also important.

vulnerable heart, a child who loves but is afraid to love. Silent prayer nourishes this deep place. It is the most important nourishment of all for people who live in community, because it is the most secret and personal.

* * *

Carlo Caretto[1] speaks of finding the desert wherever we are, in our own room, in a church, even in the middle of a crowd. I sometimes find that desert in the street between l'Arche's houses in Trosly; then I recollect myself and rediscover this tabernacle in which Jesus lives. But I also need longer times.

* * *

Often at l'Arche or elsewhere, when I am waiting for someone who is late, I get irritable. I hate wasting time. My inner motor goes on running, but isn't getting anywhere. My energy is revving but not directed. I get worse on a journey! I still have a lot to learn about using these apparently wasted moments to relax and rest, find the presence of God, live more totally in the presence of others, or simply look around like a child and wonder. I need to discover patience and even more, how to live in the moment given by God.

* * *

Two dangers lie in wait for members of a community. Either they build a protective wall for themselves—in the name of their union with God, their health or their private life—or they throw themselves helter-skelter into meetings, spilling all their emotions in the name of dialogue and sharing. The first group tend to live for themselves in a false solitude; the second tend to become dependent on others and lose their own identity. The balance between solitude and community is difficult to find.

At one time, we tended to ignore the gift of community and of sharing; now we are in danger of forgetting the gift of the inner life and the needs of the heart. To live fully in community, we must first know how to keep going and to love. The community is a spring-board, not a refuge. People who marry just because they need to are in danger of having problems. The real reason to get married is that you love each other and

[1]Carlo Caretto, *In Search of the Beyond*, Darton, Longman and Todd, London, 1975.

120

want to live and travel together, and to make each other happy. In the same way, we enter community in response to a call from God, to be what we should be, to live with others and to build something with them. But this demands that we have our own roots. Otherwise, we will not have the inner consciousness that helps us distinguish the will of God and the true needs of the community from our own instincts, fears and needs. We will speak not to give life, but to free ourselves or to prove something; we will act with and for others, not for their growth, but because we need to be doing something. To grow in human ways and inner freedom, we need both sharing and communal prayer, and solitude, reflection, inwardness and personal prayer.

* * *

Henry Nouwen[1] shows that some people find an opposition between solitude and community. Either solitude is equated with private life, which must be protected from the life of "generosity" which is community; or solitude is there to enable us to live community life more fully, a necessary resource if we are to become more to others.

But it is not simply that solitude is "for me" and community "for others."

"Solitude is essential to community life because in solitude we grow closer to each other. In solitude we discover each other in a way which physical presence makes difficult, if not impossible. There we recognise a bond with each other that does not depend on words, gestures or actions and that is deeper and stronger than our own efforts can create.

"Solitude and community belong together; each requires the other as do the centre and circumference of a circle. Solitude without community leads us to loneliness and despair, but community without solitude hurls us into a 'void of words and feelings' (Bonhoeffer)."[2]

* * *

Community life, with all its complexity, implies an inner attitude. Without this, it very quickly ossifies and we seek all sorts of compromises to avoid growth. This attitude is that of a

[1] *Solitude and Community*, in Worship, Jan. 1978.
[2] Third Canon of the Mass

trusting child who knows that he is only a tiny part of the universe and that he is called to live in gift and oblation where he is. The attitude implies a total confidence in God, seeking His will and pleasure at each moment. When we no longer have the heart of a child who seeks to be an instrument of peace and unity among men, we either become discouraged or want to prove ourselves. In either case, we destroy the community.

How to nourish this child's heart? That is the essential question for everyone who lives in community. Love can only feed on love. The only way to learn to love is to love. As soon as the cancer of egoism takes hold, it spreads very quickly through everyday activities. When the love that is sacrifice begins to grow, words, gestures and flesh itself are permeated with gift and communion.

The heart is nourished if it remains faithful to the heart of God.

* * *

Prayer is no more than the child resting in his Father's arm and saying "Yes."

The heart finds its nourishment in fidelity to the poor, listening to them and allowing itself to be disturbed by their prophetic presence. It finds its nourishment in fidelity to the collective conscience and structures of the community, in its continual, loving and patient "yes" to these.

* * *

Becoming bread

Some people, who cannot see what nourishment they could be bringing, refuse to become bread for others. They have no confidence that their word, their smile, their being or their prayer could nourish others and help them rediscover trust.

Others find that their own nourishment is to give from an empty basket! It is the miracle of the multiplication. "Lord, let me seek not so much to be consoled as to console." I am always completely astonished to discover that I can give a nourishing talk when I feel empty, and that I can still transmit peace when I feel anguished. Only God can perform that sort of miracle.

* * *

Sometimes I meet people who are aggressive towards their community. They blame their own mediocrity on it, claiming that it isn't nourishing enough and doesn't give them what they need. They are like children who blame their parents for everything that goes wrong. They lack maturity, inner freedom and above all, trust in themselves, Jesus and their brothers and sisters. They want a banquet with a nicely written menu, so they reject the crumbs they could have all the time. Their "ideal", their idea of the spiritual nourishment they feel they need, prevents them from seeing and eating the food God is giving them in their daily life. They cannot accept the bread that the poor people, their brothers and sisters, are offering them through their look, their friendship or their words. At the start, community can be a nourishing mother. But with time, we must all discover our own nourishment in its thousand and one activities. We may find the strength from God to discover our own wound and solitude, our cry of distress. Community can never comfort this distress; it is inherent in the human condition. But community can help us to accept it, and remind us that God responds to our cry and that we are not entirely alone. "And the Word became flesh and dwelt among us" (John 1, 14). "Fear not, for I am with you" (Isaiah 43,5). To live in community is to learn to walk alone in the desert, at night and in tears, putting our confidence in God the Father.

* * *

When the original vision of the community gets lost, when we are far from the focal point of fidelity, we can stuff ourselves with a diet of spirituality but get no nourishment from it at all. We have to become re-converted, become again like little children, and rediscover our original call and that of the community. When we question this call, doubt spreads like a cancer which can undermine us entirely. We have to know how to nourish our trust in the call.

* * *

Communal prayer and Eucharist

Communal prayer is an important nourishment. A community which prays together, which enters into silence and adoration, is bound together by the action of the Holy Spirit. God listens in a special way to the cry which rises from a community.

When we ask Him, together, for a gift or grace, He listens and grants our request. Jesus says that God will give whatever is asked in his name; all the more reason for Him to give when it is a community that asks. It seems to me that we do not yet have enough recourse to this communal prayer at l'Arche. Perhaps we are not yet simple or child-like enough. In spontaneous community prayer we sometimes feel a bit lost. It is sad, to me, that we do not use the very beautiful texts of the church, that we do not know the scriptures better. It is true that a text can lose its savour if it is used every day. But spontaneity can lose its savour too. We have to find a harmony between the texts that tradition gives us and the spontaneous prayer which springs from the heart.

* * *

Often a community stops crying to God when it has itself stopped hearing the cry of the poor, when it has become self-satisfied and found a way of life which is not too insecure. It is when we are aware of the distress and misery of our people, and of their oppression and suffering, when we see them starving and sense our own inability to do anything about it that we will cry loudly to God: "Lord, you cannot turn a deaf ear to the cry of your people; listen then to our prayer." When the community makes a covenant with poor people, their cry becomes its own.

* * *

A community must be a sign of the resurrection. But a divided community, in which everyone goes their own way, preoccupied with their own sanctification and personal projects, and without tenderness for the other, is a counter-witness. All the resentment, bitterness, sadness, rivalries, divisions, refusals to hold out a hand to "the enemy" and whispered criticisms, all the division and infidelity to the gift of the community, are profoundly wounding to its true growth in love. Divisions also show the bruises of sin, the forces of evil which are always in our hearts, ready to erupt. It is important that a community sometimes takes stock of all its infidelities. Penitential ceremonies in the presence of a priest can be important, if they are well prepared: the community's members become conscious of both their call to unity and their sin, demanding forgiveness of God and each other. It can be a moment of grace which brings hearts together.

* * *

The Eucharist links communal and personal nourishment, because it is itself both at the same time. The Eucharist is celebration, the epitome of the communal feast, because in it we relive the mystery of Jesus's gift of his own life for us. It is the time of thanksgiving for the whole community. That is why the priest says, after the consecration: "Grant that we, who are nourished by his body and blood, may be filled with his Holy Spirit and become one body, one spirit in Christ."[1] There we touch the heart of the mystery of community.

But the Eucharist is also an intimate moment when each of us is transformed through a personal meeting with Jesus. "He who eats my flesh and drinks my blood abides in me and I in him" (John 6,56). At the moment of consecration, the priest repeats Jesus's words: "Take this all of you and eat it, this is my body which will be given up for you." It is the "given up for you" which is striking. It is only when we have eaten this body that we can give ourselves to others. Only God could invent something like that.

* * *

[1] Third Canon of the Mass

5

GIFTS

AUTHORITY[1]

The role of authority can only be understood if it is seen as
one of the many gifts or ministries which we need to build
community. It is, of course, a very important gift, because the
community's growth depends to a great extent on the way it is
exercised. But too often authority is seen as the only gift
needed; the role of everyone else in the community is seen
simply as obedience to it. This, however, is an industrial or
military model of authority. It is exercised in a completely
different way in a community. The leaders do not have a
monopoly of insights and gifts; their role, on the contrary, is to
help all the community's members to exercise their own gifts
for the good of the whole. A community can only become a
harmonious whole, with "one heart, one soul, one spirit", if all
its members are exercising their own gifts fully. If the model of
their relationship to authority is worker to boss, or soldier to
officer, then there is no understanding of what community
means. When I speak of "authority" in the following pages, I
do not mean only the leader of a community, but all those who
have some responsibility over others. At l'Arche, that means
those in charge of the workshops, the houses and the garden
teams, as well as anyone in the administration, the kitchens

[1] I was greatly helped in writing this section by the many valuable
insights into authority of Robert K. Greenleaf, in his book *Servant
Leadership* (Panlist Press, New York, 1977).

and the service of welcome who has charge over the work of others. Each person has to learn how to exercise authority in a way that is right for a Christian community.

* * *

A mission from God

The people who carry responsibility in a community have received a mission which has been confided to them either by the community, which has elected them, or by a superior, who has appointed them. So they are accountable to them. But this mission has also been received from God. We cannot assume responsibility towards other people without His help, for, as St. Paul says: "there is no authority except from God, and those that exist have been instituted by God" (Romans 13,1). Anyone who carries authority which comes from God must be accountable to God. That is the limitation and the scope of human authority.

Authority is there to help the freedom and growth of individuals. It is a work of love. Just as God watches over his children to see that they grow in love and truth, so the people responsible for a community must be at the service of God and individuals, so that they too can grow in love and truth.

This is a huge responsibility. But it is beautiful too, because the people set in authority have the assurance that God will send the insight, strength and gifts they need to accomplish the task. That is why those in authority have to do more than refer to those who appointed them, as the secretary of an association would do. They must refer to God and discover the divine light in their own hearts. I am a great believer in the grace of the moment: God will always come to the aid of people in authority if they are humble and try in truth to serve.

People in authority must take heed of what others think. But they must not be imprisoned by these views. They have a responsibility before God and so have no right to compromise, deceive or be instruments of injustice.

* * *

The people who carry final authority in communities are always, in a sense, alone. Even if there is a council, they will have to take some decisions by themselves. This loneliness is their cross, but it is also the guarantee of presence, light and the strength of God. That is why they, more than anyone else in the community, must have time to be alone with God. It is in these moments of solitude that inspiration is born in them and they will sense what direction to take. They must have confidence in these intuitions, especially if they are accompanied by a deep peace. But they must also confirm them, by sharing them with the most discerning members of the community and then with its council.

Faced with difficult decisions about the future, they must of course reason and reflect, having all the information available. But at the end of the day, because of the complexity of the problems and the impossibility of forseeing every detail, they must, having assimilated everything, rely on the deep intuitions which come to them when they are alone. This is the only way that people with authority can acquire the freedom which will allow them to go forward and take decisions without fearing the consequences.

* * *

Being a servant

There are different ways of exercising authority and command. There is the military model, the industrial model and the community model. The general's goal is victory; the factory manager's goal is profit. The goal of the leader of a community is the growth of individuals in love and truth.

Leaders of a community have a double mission. They must keep their eyes and those of the community fixed on what is essential, on the fundamental aims of the community. They must give direction, so that the community doesn't get lost in small wrangles, which are secondary and incidental. At l'Arche, those with responsibility have always to remind people that the community exists essentially to welcome handicapped people and help them grow, in the spirit of the Beatitudes. The members of a community of prayer have always to be reminded that the demands of work are subordinate to those of prayer. The mission of people in authority is to keep the community in touch with the essential.

But their mission is also to create an atmosphere of mutual confidence, peace and joy among the community's members.

128

Through their relationship with each person, through the trust shown in them, they will lead each member to trust the others. Human beings grow best in a relaxed environment built on mutual confidence. When there is rivalry, jealousy and suspicion, and where people are blocked against each other, there can be no community, no growth and no life of witness.

* * *

Different people exercise authority in different ways, according to their own temperaments. Some people are leaders and have a creativity which gives them a vision of the future: they lead from the front. Others are more shy and humble: they walk among the others and make excellent coordinators. The essential, for all people with authority, is that they are servants before they are bosses. People who assume responsibility to prove something, because they tend to be dominating and controlling, because they need to see themselves at the top or because they are looking for privileges and prestige, will always exercise their responsibility badly. They must first want to be servants.

Some communities choose their leaders for their administrative ability or ascendancy over others. But leaders should never be chosen for their natural qualities; they should be chosen only because they have shown that they put the interests of the community above their own. People who want to serve the community and others are worth more, even if they are shy and lack the ability to command, than people who are "capable" but bound up in themselves.

* * *

The people who carry responsibility best are those who receive it as a mission of God and lean on His strength and the gifts of the Holy Spirit. They will feel poor and incapable, but they will always act humbly for the good of the community. They will have the community's confidence, for it will sense that they trust not in themselves and their own vision, but in God. The community will sense that they have no need to prove anything, that they are not seeking anything for themselves and that their vision isn't clouded by their own problems. It will sense that they are willing to disappear when the moment comes.

* * *

The first quality needed by those who carry responsibility is a love for all the members of the community and a concern for their growth. This implies that they also carry the weaknesses of others. The members of the community can sense very quickly if those with responsibility love and trust them, are there to prove their authority and impose their own vision, or are just seeking to please.

The model of authority for all Christians is Jesus—Jesus who washed the feet of his disciples, the Good Shepherd who gave up his life for his flock. It is not the hired man who acted purely in his own interests.

* * *

Stay confident!

Sometimes at l'Arche I can feel a bit overwhelmed by problems. A handicapped person or an assistant may be very unwell. One of the houses may be struggling. A group of assistants may be united against something I feel to be essential. There may be divisions in the community, especially between the professionally-oriented, who want more competence, and the spiritually-oriented, who want a more religious life. These sorts of things turn me grey.

But it doesn't do for me to take myself too seriously. I have to remember that I don't have to solve all problems single-handed. First of all, there are several of us who share responsibility. But, most important, God has promised to help us. We are His servants and the community's; we can only do what we can, and God will do the rest. So we shouldn't get too het up. We have to be aware of what is going on, and explain the problems clearly to the council or others with responsibility, if this becomes necessary. So we have to discern calmly what has to be done and act accordingly, taking small steps forward, even if the horizon is blurred.

People with responsibility will be faced by many complex problems. They must keep the heart of a child, confident that Jesus will always come to their help in their weakness. They have to put their worries into God's hands and then do whatever they can.

No one will be happy in the community if the responsible

people are always preoccupied, serious and closed in on themselves. Responsibility is certainly a cross which has to be picked up each day. But we have to learn to carry it lightly. The secret is to stay young, open and capable of wonder. And the best way to do that is to stay open to the Holy Spirit, the youth of the Father.

* * *

There is often a danger of failing to take a decision because we are afraid of it. But not to take a decision is in fact to take one. People with responsibility certainly need patience; they shouldn't act in the flush of anger. They have to listen, find out the facts and take their time. But, after prayer and discussion, they also have to be able to take decisions and not let themselves be controlled by circumstances or past events.

* * *

The people who carry responsibility well are those who engender confidence and hope.

* * *

The danger of pride

I increasingly see how difficult it is to exercise authority in a community. We are so inclined to want authority for the honour, prestige or admiration that comes with it, or to prove something. Inside each of us is a little tyrant who wants power and the associated prestige, who wants to dominate and be superior. We are frightened of criticism, of being controlled. We feel we are the only ones to see the truth—and that, sometimes, in the name of God. We interfere with the work of others, taking charge of everything and jealously guarding our authority. The others are reduced to simply carrying out our ideas, as if they were incapable of making judgements themselves. We only allow freedom when it doesn't challenge our own authority and we can control it. We want our ideas to be put into action, and straight away. So the community becomes "our" project.

All these tendencies can very easily filter into the exercise of authority, to one degree or another. And Christians can sometimes hide these tendencies behind a mask of virtue, doing what they do for "good" reasons. There is nothing more terrible than a tyrant using religion as his cover. I know my own tendencies towards this and I have to struggle against them constantly.

It is important that the limits of individual power in a community are clearly understood and even written down. A father so quickly goes beyond his proper power over his children, wanting them to turn out according to his own ideas; he so quickly fails to take their freedom and their wishes into account.

It is not easy for people in authority to find the mean between too much command and too little. The dangers of pride and the desire to dominate are so great for all leaders that they need limits set to their power, and systems of control which help them to be objective and remain truly at the service of the community.

* * *

Rivalry for power between members of the community and jealousy of the others' radiance is a terrible force for destruction. A united community is like a rock; a community which is divided against itself rapidly destroys itself. Women tend to be rivals in love, men, in power.

Even the apostles around Jesus, sometimes behind his back, argued about who was the greatest among them (Mark 10, 41;9,34). St Luke says they were talking about this during the last supper. Is that why Jesus got up from the table and washed their feet?

Rivalry between members of a community often becomes more apparent when there is a vote for a position of responsibility. There can also be rivalry over who is the most spiritual and intellectual. These struggles for power and influence are deeply rooted in our human hearts. We are afraid we will no longer exist if we do not win the vote, or a certain position. We are so quick to equate function and person, popularity and quality of being.

* * *

No authority is free from over-hasty judgements which wound people and catch them up in a vicious circle of anger and sadness. Unity grows from the soil of humility, which is the safeguard against schisms and division. The spirit of evil is

132

powerless against it. And it is the spirit of evil which creates deceit, illusion and disturbance, and provokes pride.

* * *

The servant of the weakest

The people who assume responsibility should remember that, in the perspective of the Gospel, it is the poor people who are the most precious and close to God, not the leaders. It is the poor people whom God has chosen to confound the strong and who are at the heart of Christian community. The whole ministry of government must be geared to the poor people and their growth in love. "The greatest", says Jesus, "is the one who humbles himself and becomes like a little child" (Luke 9,46-48; Matthew 18,1-5).

* * *

People with responsibility must always be concerned for the minorities in a community and those who have no voice, listening to them and interpreting for them. The leaders must defend individuals because the interests of the individual must never be sacrificed to those of the group. A community is always built around people; people should not be shaped to suit community.

* * *

Sharing responsibility

One of the most important things for people in authority is to be clear about their priorities. If they lose themselves in a thousand details, they are in danger of losing the vision. They have to keep their eyes fixed firmly on the essential. The best authority is the one which does very little itself but reminds others of this essential in their activities and their life, calls them to assume responsibilities, supports them, confirms them and directs them.

* * *

People with responsibility must always share their work, even if others do it less well than they do or in a different way. It is always easier to do things ourselves than to teach others to do them. People with responsibility who fall into the trap of wanting to do everything themselves are in danger of becoming isolated.

* * *

People who are given responsibility must at the same time be given the means of assuming it. Over-protection is finally a refusal to share responsibility. People have a right to make their own mistakes and fall on their faces. Doing everything for them may protect them from set-backs, but it also prevents them from succeeding—however irrelevant the concepts of "success' and "failure" are in community. People cannot be left to carry responsibility alone. They need someone who counsels, supports, encourages and directs them. They should not be left to muddle through situations and tensions which are too difficult for them to handle. They need someone to whom they can talk freely, who understands and confirms them in responsibility. They need a discreet presence who does not judge, who has experience in human affairs and who instils confidence. Otherwise, they will be in danger of cracking. Jesus promised another Paraclete to his disciples, and we all have to be paracletes for the others, responsive to their call. The cross of responsibility is sometimes heavy and we need a friend who understands, an older brother or sister, to make our task less onerous.

* * *

When a community starts, it is the founder who decides everything. But gradually brothers and sisters arrive and bonds are created. Then the founder asks their advice. It is no longer he who dictates what should be happening; he listens to others. A communal spirit is born. The founder begins to discover the gift of each of the others. He discovers that others are more able than he is in certain ways and that they have gifts which he doesn't. So he entrusts more and more to others, learning to die to himself so that the others can live more fully. He remains the link and the reference, a coordinator who confirms the others in their responsibilities and oversees the maintenance of the spirit and unity. At moments of crisis, he will still be called on to assert his authority, because the ultimate responsibility rests with him; he must, when discipline is failing, recall the others to their responsibilities. His authority becomes remote, but still very present until the day he disappears and another takes his place. Then his task is done. His work will continue; his role has been to disappear.

There is an analogy with the authority of parents. At the start, they do everything for their children, but gradually they become friends with whom their children can discuss things; they can even become their children's children when they are old. Parents have to guard against a possessiveness which stifles the life that is growing in their children. In the same way, the founder of a community must learn to withdraw gradually and not to cling to his authority.

* * *

At the start, the founder bases his actions on his own vision. Gradually the people who join him become one body with all the life and inevitable tensions that that must bring. Then the founder can no longer behave as if he were the only one to have a vision. He must listen to the community, and respect its life and vision. The role of the founder is to understand the life of the community and allow it to flourish under his guidance.

* * *

Perhaps the hardest thing a founder has to do is accept that the vision of others may reflect the community and its fundamental goals more clearly and truly than does his own.

* * *

At l'Arche, we have a council of seventeen people, elected by assistants who have been with us for more than two years. This council meets for a morning each week to share about the orientations of the community and take major decisions. I have learned a lot from these meetings. I have learned about the difficulties of sharing and together searching not for our own will but for the will of the community and of God. We so quickly become possessive and emotionally involved. I have been helped to discover how I myself have to grow, to become more open to the Spirit and more objective. It seems to me now that all people who carry authority should have a meeting like this, where they can discern together, where authority is shared, supported and directed and where they can grow to be better able to carry responsibility together.

* * *

People must remain faithful to their community's structures. It would be a big mistake if I took a decision which should have been referred to the council. The process of decision-making here is longer and it is sometimes hard for me to restrain my own "inspirations." But this is the way we come to mature decisions together.

* * *

I am discovering more and more how hard it is to carry authority. I very quickly come up against a hard and defensive aspect of myself. I sometimes find it difficult to link listening to people and compassion with firmness, objectivity and the hope that they will grow. I am too often either timid and indecisive, letting people go their own way, or rigid and legalistic. Each day I have to acquire wisdom in responsibility, as well as strength and patience. My brothers and sisters on the council of l'Arche have helped me a lot. But I have a long way to go yet!

* * *

One of the essential qualities of people with responsibility is an ability to listen to everyone and not just to their friends and admirers. They have to know where people are and to create bonds with them which are true and, if possible, warm. People who carry responsibility badly hide behind prestige, power, the rulebook and their own commands; they listen only to their friends. They talk a lot but don't stop to listen to how others are receiving what they say. They do not, above all, try to understand other people's deep needs, aspirations, difficulties and sufferings; they do not understand the way God has called others. People with authority who do not know how to listen to those who disagree with them, or to grasp the grain of truth hidden among the weeds of discontent, are living in insecurity. They would do well to allow the members of the community to discuss their view of how authority should be exercised with the friendly outsider we mentioned earlier.

* * *

One reason that people with responsibility fail to listen is that they fail to see the community as it really is. They become lazy optimists; "Everything will sort itself out" becomes their slogan. Basically, they are frightened of acting, or feel incompetent in the face of reality. It is hard to be constantly conscious of reality, because it is distubing. But it sharpens our awareness too. An aware authority is one which seeks to understand, prays and cries out to God. Its thirst for truth will grow and God will answer its cry. But at the same time, it has to be very patient, a true friend to time.

* * *

Bad leaders are concerned only with rules and regulations. They do not try to understand how these affect people. It is easy to use the law to cover an inability to understand and listen. We impose rules when we are frightened of people.

* * *

People with responsibility have to avoid the temptation of listening only to people who talk well and know how to win them over, carefully avoiding established structures.

* * *

It is important for people in authority to listen to the young people who enter the community. Their call, inspiration and wishes can reveal a lot. The people in authority have to know how to listen to them with interest and marvel at God's work in them. Their call can show what the community should be and its failings as well. In his rule, St. Benedict says that each time there is something important to discuss, the Abbot should call the whole community together to get the advice of his brothers. And "God often inspires the youngest to make the best suggestions."[1]

* * *

Don't hide!

People with responsibility are in danger of throwing up barriers between themselves and those for whom they are responsible. They give the impression of always being busy. They impress others with the size of their car or their office. They give the impression that they are superior, or at least the most important person around. These leaders are afraid and create fear in others. They keep their distance because they are insecure. Truly responsible people are open to others. They don't use a car, because walking gives others the chance to meet them and talk to them like friends. They do not hide in their

[1] *Rule of St Benedict*, chapter III

offices, and so stay vulnerable to criticism. People in authority should always stay close to those for whom they are responsible and encourage true and simple meetings. If they stay aloof, they cannot know their people or their people's needs.

* * *

It is important for people in authority to reveal themselves as they are and share their difficulties and weaknesses. If they hide these, people may see them as an unattainable model. They have to be seen as fallible and human, but at the same time trusting and trying to grow.

* * *

It is no bad thing either if people with responsibility do a bit of manual work, whether this is washing up or cooking the occasional meal. This keeps their feet on the ground and ensures that they get their hands dirty. It creates new relationships; those who work with them see them as people and not just as functions.

* * *

Some people in authority will always need to have someone close to them who knows how to knock them off their pedestal, tease them and sometimes give them a kick in the pants. They so often meet either adulation or aggression. They can very quickly shut themselves up in their role because they are afraid or believe themselves to be a little god; then they will lose touch with reality. They need people who can gently tease them, who refuse to take them too seriously, who see who they really are and bring them back to earth. Of course, they must have confidence in these people and know that they are loved by them.

* * *

A personalised authority

Many people seem to have a strange concept of authority and responsibility. They are afraid of them and of taking them on. Authority seems for them to be cut off from tenderness and friendship; they see it as nothing but bad and bullying. Perhaps they had an authoritarian father, neither tender nor trusting. Perhaps too this is one of the ills of our times; the tendency everywhere seems to be to cut authority off from love.

True authority is exercised in the context of justice for all, with special attention to the weakest people, who cannot defend themselves and are part of the oppressed minority. This is an authority ready to give its life, which does not accept any compromise with evil, deceit and the forces of oppression. A family or community authority, as well as having this sense of justice and truth, needs personal relationships, sensitivity in its action and the ability to listen, trust and forgive. None of this, of course, excludes moments of firmness.

* * *

At the same time, and perhaps for the same reasons, many people confuse authority and the power of efficiency, as if the first role of people with responsibility was to take decisions, command effectively and so exercise power. But their role is first of all to be a reference, provide security, confirm, support, encourage and guide.

* * *

Some communities refuse to have anyone in charge of them at all. They want to be governed democratically, through consensus, with no coordinator, "father" or "elder brother." It would be silly to say that this is impossible. But from my experience of l'Arche, it seems to me that the members of a community need someone to whom they can refer and with whom they can have a personal relationship. People can reject all personal authority because they feel that it is always subjective and to do with personal prestige; for them, only consensus allows for objectivity.

It is true that consensus or collegiate government does allow for greater objectivity. It is also true that none of us is more intelligent than all of us together. A group will make juster rules than an individual. But, on the other hand, a group, because it is always objective, cannot allow for exceptions to its rule. In a community which has to do with the growth of people, there has to be an authority which can speak to individuals and establish trusting relationships with them. Communities which refuse the idea of a "father" or "elder brother" are often made up of people who are young—at least in community life—and oriented towards effective and absorbing work. An older community, which knows the weaknesses of its members and which welcomes vulnerable people of all sorts, realises its need for an authority which is personal, loving and trusting.

The quality of life of a community can decline very quickly; weakness, fragility, egoism and apathy are quick to appear. The role of the "father" or "elder brother" is to encourage, support, forgive and sometimes direct and restore order, so that the quality of life remains high. We enter community not because we are perfect, objective and intelligent, but because we want to grow towards a truer wisdom and love. And if this human growth is to be possible, there must be someone who confirms, supports, brings security and helps people regain confidence in themselves so that they can walk with greater courage and trust. Community questions have also, of course, to be settled through communal discernment, and people with responsibility help with this. But there are always those whose human, spiritual or psychological weaknesses make them exceptional. They need to find another, compassionate human heart, to which they can open in confidence. We don't open our heart to a group; we open it to an individual.

* * *

Aristotle speaks of *epiki* as one of the virtues of the leader. It is this which enables him to interpret the law. The people who make that law cannot foresee every case. The leader, faced with the exceptional case, has a sense of justice and of the needs of individuals which enables him to act as the lawgivers themselves would have acted in the circumstances.

A group will always act according to the precepts of justice and the law. It is impossible in a community to take each decision on its individual merits—that would lead to all sorts of comparisons, jealousies, claims and counter-claims. There must be a rule. But at the same time, there must be the possibility of allowing for exceptions to that rule. A personalised authority will always put the good of the individual before that of the group and before the law; this authority will show compassion and goodness towards the weak and be able to deal with the exceptional cases.

All this, of course, presupposes a loving authority which is at the service of individuals!

* * *

How to learn to be a father? I am sure that we can only be a father if we are conscious of ourself as a son. We can only command if we know how to obey. Jesus is the lamb before he is the shepherd. After all, his authority comes from the fact that he is his Father's son.

* * *

There is a crisis of authority at the moment, partly perhaps because some psychoanalytic doctrines tend to undermine the role of the father. But we cannot accept a law unless we first have confidence in the person in whom it is incarnate. Delinquents rebel against the law because they have not made the transition from reliance on the tenderness of their mother to trust in their father; that is why they find authority unbearable. We can only accept a law if it is incarnate in a person who is able to forgive, take account of exceptions to the rule and, above all, to understand and have mercy.

* * *

Father Leon, founder of La Pondrière community in Brussels, has said that when no one carries responsibility in a community, its aggression is directed against its weakest members. Something is always going badly in a community and it is important that the people with responsibility recognise that one of their roles is to receive and channel this aggression.

* * *

Attitudes to authority

Some people in community say that they cannot obey authority unless they have trust—and they mean complete trust—in those in whom authority is vested. There is something infantile in that; it is like the attitude of children who obey their parents until the day they discover that their parents have human failings.

Authority in a community is not all-powerful. There are always limits to it. The responsibility of the leader should be well-defined in the community's constitution, and that constitution must also guarantee the right of all members to express their concerns about the way authority is exercised. If it does not do this, the door is open to division and dissent.

When people say that they can only obey an authority in which they have total confidence, they are looking for an ideal father. Their demand excludes any authority elected for a limited period; it excludes any real sharing of responsibility. We have to learn how to obey people who have been appointed or elected to responsibility according to the constitution, even if we do not feel any great friendship or affection for them. If we can feel this, so much the better. But it is unrealistic to expect it. If the condition of obedience is emotional trust, the way is open to anarchy and the possible death of the community.

It is not necessary to have total trust in the individuals with authority. But we should trust the people who have elected them and the constitution, the community's structures, dialogue, and God, who is watching over the community. He knows how to use even those who appear incompetent; He knows how to give them the grace to achieve their tasks without too many mistakes. We have to believe that the people with responsibility will find the grace for the moment.

* * *

If there is no obedience, the community cannot exist. But this obedience is not something external and servile. It is an internalised support of legitimate authority, of the structures of decision—making and of the communal conscience of the community. It is a search for a communal vision. It is a belief in the principles on which the community's life and action are based.

If this communal conscience is rejected, there will be division. We create division when we believe that we are the only ones to see the truth, when we set ourselves up as saviours against authority, when we reject the legal structures and when we want to prove we are right.

Of course people in authority can make mistakes, and of course structures can be defensive and stifling. Those in authority can seek to defend their privileges and behave like hired men instead of servants. It is then that a higher authority must intervene, and that an effort must be made to recast the structures, using constitutional means to hold discussions with the people who carry responsibility. If they still refuse to change, if there is no sign of evolution or desire for dialogue, then non-violent means must be used to make them change or evolve. The Marxist tactic is to expose the weakness of legitimate authority to bring it down, and create anarchy which is succeeded by a totalitarianism founded on police power. That is the tactic of confrontation. Members of a community who do not carry responsibility must always feel personally responsible when those in authority are closing in on themselves. The members must tackle them if necessary, but in friendly dialogue. Those with responsibility in community are often criticised behind their backs; people are often too cowardly to speak to them directly.

* * *

"We beseech you, brethren, to respect those who labour among you and are over you in the Lord and admonish you, and to esteem them very highly in love because of their work. Be at peace among yourselves. And we exhort you, brethren, admonish the idle, encourage the faint-hearted, help the weak, be patient with them all. See that none of you repays evil with evil, but always seek to do good to one another and to all. Rejoice always, pray constantly, give thanks in all circumstances; for this is the will of God in Jesus Christ for you. Do not quench the Spirit, do not despise prophesying, but test everything; hold fast what is good, abstain from every form of evil" (I Thessalonians 5,12-22).

* * *

People in authority often become the focus for all sorts of personal and community discontents. Someone has to be the target for blame! We often expect too much of them; we seek an ideal father who knows everything, has all the gifts of a leader and can resolve all problems. We want an ideal leader who brings us security; we feel insecure when we realise that no one has all the gifts we are looking for. And so we reject the leader who fails to live up to our ideal.

We are often too dependent on the people with responsibility. We look constantly for their approval. We become servile. And then, discontented with our own servility, we criticise them behind their back. The leader often attracts either servility or aggression.

* * *

The relationship that people have with authority is often linked to the relationship they had as children with their parents. When this was difficult, when the parents lacked respect for their children's freedom and imposed their own wishes, the children can be left with a lasting anger and suspicion of all authority. Their relationships with it will be coloured by these emotions and psychological blocks. As soon as the leader intervenes, they will rebel against him and reject his command. They want him to approve of everything they do. As soon as he seems to question them, they clam up. They often have problems in seeing the person behind the position, who is not all-powerful and all-knowing, but equally does have his own gift to offer and has to grow to use that gift better each day. They often cannot admit that authority too has its failings. The relationship is a complicated one, and it is hard to dialogue in simplicity and truth, because everything is coloured by childish fear and attitudes.

The leader is very often put on a pedestal and idealised. But that can simply mean that he is an easier target for criticism. People are careful not to aim for the heart, though; it is enough to wound him in the leg. His death, after all, would be a catastrophe, because then someone else would have to take on the job and that is not what his critics want.

* * *

The hardest step of all in human growth may well be that from the child's dependence on and aggression towards its parents, to a friendship and dialogue with them, which recognises their grace and gifts. We become adult when we have acquired an inner freedom and a real capacity for judgement, and when we have fully accepted the gift of others and allowed ourselves to be touched by the light that is in them. That is the passage from dependence to interdependence, and the people in authority should play their part in helping us achieve it. But the passage to a new inner freedom cannot be made without cries and anguish.

* * *

To know how to dialogue with and obey authority is an important quality in community life.

* * *

The sign of forgiveness

Forgiveness is at the heart of Christian community and the leaders must be the sign and model of this forgiveness. They must know how to forgive all the aggression and apathy that are focused on them, seventy times seven. Each day, they have to relearn how to meet people as people and let people meet them in the same way, knowing that the road by which anyone finds a true relationship with authority is a long one. Through forgiveness, the leaders assume their own fears and defences, which lead them to be aggressive towards, or flee from, others. To forgive is to be open and relaxed, understanding and patient with those who are aggressive.

Stephen Verney sums it up well: faced with aggression or servility, "the leader can react in a number of ways. He can focus the attention of the group upon its purpose, and thus relieve the pressure on himself. He can make warm personal relationships with each individual member of the group, while retaining his command over the group as a whole. Both the tactics may be beneficial and promote the health of the group. But if he aspires to enable the group to live the life of the new age, then alongside and in conjunction with these two styles of leadership he must adopt a third, which is to be one step ahead of the group in this very process of forgiveness which is its essence. That is to say, he must become more aware of the good and evil that interlock both in himself and in the group, and he must pass through the experience of death and resurrection by which they may be unlocked and transformed. This he will have to do not once, but continuously. As Jesus puts it, hyperbolically but realistically, he must 'take up his cross daily'."[1]

* * *

In the same way, the leader must be very patient with the slowness and mediocrity of his community. By the grace of his position, he may have a more comprehensive vision; he may understand its needs better and more rapidly than his brothers and sisters; he may have a better sense of its evolution and of God's purpose for it, and of the urgency of being more true and faithful. But others can be expected to go more slowly. The leader should not hustle them or impose his own vision; still less should he make them feel guilty. Through his tender-

[1] Stephen Verney, *Into the New Age*, Fontana/Collins, 1976, p. 120-121

ness, gentleness, patience, acceptance and above all, humility, he should engender a spirit of confidence. Then the others, in their turn and in their own time, will evolve, not according to his vision, but according to the vision of God for the community, and will be able to listen, forgive and respect each others' rhythm. I very much like Jacob's response to Esau when Esau invites him to journey with him: "My Lord knows that the children are frail and that the flocks and herds giving suck are a care to me; and that if they are overdriven for one day, all the flocks will die. Let my Lord pass on before his servant, and I will lead on slowly, according to the pace of the cattle which are before me and according to the pace of the children" (Genesis 33,13-14).

* * *

Carrying the community

One of the roles of the person with responsibility in a community is to understand and contain the group as a whole. "By 'holding' the group in this way", says Stephen Verney, "he provides a secure container (room to move, time to face things, space to change), within which it is safe to test out new ways of dealing with the world, corresponding to the safe containment and control provided by the mother to the foetus and later to the infant, and by the mother to the mother/child complex and later to the family."[1]

A leader who is himself insecure, afraid and anxious about his own authority will not allow the community to evolve. He will have a static model for it. The leader has to be free enough, and have enough confidence in the group and himself, to allow the group's life to evolve. To achieve this, he must not let himself be overwhelmed by everyday concerns; he must keep the distance he needs to grow and act on new inspirations. The leader is not simply the guardian of the law, although that is one aspect of his role. He is there to guarantee the freedom and growth of individuals according to the inspiration of God. Authentic inspirations are those which help build the community according to its fundamental goals, even if they are not always recognised straight away. In fact, these

[1] op. cit.

146

inspirations can often disturb the community, because of the challenge they bring. But these are necessary challenges, which remind the community of the essential. The leader must recognise their authenticity and help the community to recognise it too.

* * *

Even very limited and fragile people, if they can work with a leadership that has vision, compassion and firmness, can do marvellous things. They participate in the leader's vision and they benefit from his gifts. The wealth of a community lies in the fact that all its members can share the qualities and gifts of the others.

It is sometimes difficult for those who carry responsibility at a lower level to fit harmoniously into the whole. They are answerable to those immediately above them—as indeed is everyone who carries responsibility, up to the director who is accountable to the Board of Directors. But it is not always easy for people in the middle range of responsibility to see when they can take initiatives on their own and when they need to refer to their immediate superior, get his opinion and recognise his authority. Some people refuse to discuss with their immediate superior, feeling more free to do what they want without this control; they act as if they were in sole charge. Others take the completely opposite line: they are so afraid of authority that they refer the last detail upwards, becoming servile and taking no real responsibility themselves. We have to find the middle way between these two extremes, assuming our responsibility fully before God and referring truthfully to him and to the next person up the line. This demands an open heart, which is not trying to prove anything.

* * *

I discover more and more the marvellous way in which responsibility leads to spiritual growth. Of course it is a cross and there is the danger of seeing it as something deserved which brings prestige and advantages. But if we are aware of the gravity of responsibility and what it means to carry people, and if we accept the cross with all its implications, this is a marvellous way to grow.

But if we are to carry our cross lightly, with patience and wisdom, we have to cling to the spirit of God. More than anyone else, we need time with our God. We will lose peace if we do not take this perspective; we will lose the light if we do not have time to listen.

Solomon's prayer should be the prayer of everyone with responsibility: "Give thy servant therefore an understanding mind to govern thy people, that I may discern between good and evil" (I Kings 3,9).

* * *

THE GIFT OF THE SHEPHERD

At the start of human life, the child receives everything from his parents—nourishment, bodily care and above all security. Their love and gift of themselves nourish and awaken his heart. Then the child grows and they give him language and supervise the awakening of his intelligence. They transmit a religious and moral tradition; they answer their child's first questions.

But gradually he discovers that his parents are not enough. The teacher feeds his intelligence; the priest or man of God helps him grow in prayer and the knowledge of God. As different aspects of the child are stimulated he discovers different references and different forms of authority. The parents' role becomes more specific: they teach him to live in the community of the family, with brothers and sisters, and they pass on a tradition and a sense of what is and isn't done. The priest forms the conscience and secret part of the person, where the seeds of the eternal are sown. This part can be quite closed to the parents, who have no right to enter it. If the child wishes to divulge his secret, they must receive this with great respect. Teachers at school are different again. They help the child discover the meaning of the universe and of human history, the history of salvation.

* * *

In the same way, at the start of a community there is a father who assumes more or less all the functions. He can be at the same time the father of the community and its authority, the spiritual father or shepherd and the master of the intelligence. But gradually these functions are diversified. The leader has to help people find the priest or shepherd who will guide them in their secret; he must also give place to a teacher. (I distinguish the leader of the community from the shepherd or spiritual director, but his role evolves with the spiritual growth of individuals. At first, they need a shepherd – father who gradually becomes a spiritual companion, a counsellor and then a witness).

* * *

We should be wary of people who call themselves shepherds or spiritual counsellors without having received the mission or authority for this. They can tend to want spiritual power without being subject to any controls themselves.

* * *

Some communities fall into the trap of seeing the leader, the prophet, the spiritual director and the therapist as one and the same person. Then this person becomes an all-powerful shepherd. But it is dangerous for him to be at the same time the community's leader and the person who guides the spiritual conscience of individuals.

If he does have these two roles, he is in danger of using his spiritual power to manipulate people for the smooth running of the community. He no longer seeks to help people to be faithful to God in their own way; he starts from the premise that they have to work for the community. That is a situation which can lead to all sorts of abuse.

In the same way, the community's members can trap the leader. Their confidences bind them to him and make the proper exercise of authority very difficult. They can even convince him that no one else can understand or help them. Then he is trapped by a sort of emotional blackmail. The person in authority must not be afraid to tell members of the community that he cannot help with their emotional or spiritual life. His role is to help them find their place in the community and to do their work well.

A father is neither a psychotherapist nor a priest. These areas of responsibility should not be confused.

* * *

I am sometimes a bit worried by communities which are carried by a single strong shepherd or a solidly united team of shepherds. As these communities have no traditions, no history and no constitutional control by a recognised legal authority, there is hardly any check on their activities. The leaders may develop a taste for their role, seeing themselves as indispensable and so unconsciously dominating others. There is also the risk of mixing community and spiritual power. It is good and useful if these spiritual shepherds quickly hand over direction of the community to someone else, so that they can be freer to exercise their gift of priest or shepherd.

* * *

A shepherd should never become all-powerful. He should never be put on a pedestal as a saint, prophet or holder of power. The greatest danger for any shepherd or leader is to believe that he is always right, and that God is with him. All men are fallible. Weak people can tend to seek security by deifying their shepherd. This is unhealthy and wrong. It is their insecurity which makes them want to turn their shepherd into a saint who will instruct them in everything.

All men are a mixture of good and evil, light and darkness. The true shepherd is humble, knows his limitations, doesn't interfere where he shouldn't and respects the gifts and charism of others. He also knows how to disappear. He carries the secret of individuals, their bonds with God, but he leaves others to help them find their place in the community.

* * *

In the council at l'Arche, we were recently talking about our need for people to support young assistants. Hubert was saying that we had to distinguish between two sorts of people. The first sees how people carry out their responsibilities, supports them, guides them and if necessary gives them direction. Their role is needed for people to assume their responsibilities. The second sort should be able to listen to deeper needs. It is better that they have no power or authority over people. If they had, they might not be sufficiently objective. There is a third function, too, which has to do with calling people to greater generosity, so that they can assume new responsibilities. These distinctions are valuable.

* * *

Sometimes, life appears perfectly clear-cut and we are peaceful. We seem to hear God calling us to make a covenant with Him and the poor. At these times, it is important to talk with a "witness" about the light which shines in us, warms us and gives us certainty. This witness—a shepherd, priest, a man of

God—will be able, from personal experience, to counsel us on how to respond to the call. He will also be able to confirm it. He can assure us that it is not an illusion, that our feelings are real and that we can follow the call and be faithful.

We need a witness and a spiritual counsellor if we are to grow and even to survive the times of anguish and darkness which are inevitable in community life. The people who confirmed our first call can remind us later of the covenant and the light. They call us to fidelity. We all need someone who will carry us through our nights and days, our winters and summers and our times of darkness and clarity. We all need someone who knows the secret of our hearts.

* * *

I am struck by how difficult it is for many people truly to discern. In the past, judgements were made according to the law and objective criteria; people obeyed and that was it. Now, discernment is increasingly made by subjective criteria. People gauge their own emotions, and if they feel troubled, they think this is because they are not acting according to God's will. We are passing from objectivity and the rule of law to subjectivity. People seem to be forgetting that there is a huge difference between the peace which is a gift of God and surpasses all understanding and peace in the psychological sense. If we are living in a dream or illusion, or have certain psychological blocks, we should not be surprised that we become troubled when someone brings us face to face with reality. Yet sometimes we have to lose psychological peace if we are to live in true peace. Divine peace often grows from humiliation and acceptance of a psychological problem. It is a gift of God which springs from our inner selves and a desire to serve our brothers and sisters. It helps us to carry our cross.

In the same way, people who are searching for their vocation are sometimes so taken up by their own small concerns that they no longer hear the cry of those who suffer or the call of the poor. We often discover our own call only when we listen to the call of others.

* * *

These times are also characterised by a struggle in many people between a desire for independence and an acceptance of interdependence. Some modern psychology seems to tell us that we have to become free of the father, as if we would then be totally independent in our thought, judgement and emotional life. But often, when we believe ourselves to be free of the father figure, we are in fact influenced by, and so dependent on, the currents of thought around us. It is not easy to know when and how to be free. The important thing is not freedom for its own sake, but freedom to love and serve better.

* * *

There is an increasing need for shepherds who help people go beyond their search for psychological peace and their own identity, to listen to the call of God and of those in distress, and to enter into covenant with them.

* * *

The priest-shepherd, spiritual counsellor and witness must understand the human heart. But they must also and above all understand the ways of God, and how the Holy Spirit, the master of love, is leading people. Psychology is helpful as far as it goes, in its aim to bring a certain psychological freedom. But men and women of God help others to live with their psychological blocks and to grow in the will of God and in love for Jesus and brothers and sisters. They help them to do this in fidelity and humility, in the certainty that this is one of the best ways to make the blocks disappear. They help people to stay in the light of God.

* * *

The witnesses of the grace of God and the secret of the individual are those who can help people discern at the great turning-points of their lives. They discern in the light of the gifts the individual has been given. That is why it is important to trust them, not only at times of crisis, when we are searching for security and consolation, but also at times of light and grace.

* * *

It is the men and women of God who help us discover the meaning of our setbacks and how to use them constructively. When we are going through difficult times in community life, and feel rejected, these people remind us: "Don't worry; it's just a difficult moment. It's a time of death—but don't you know that you have to die with Christ in order to rise again with him? Wait for the dawn. Be patient. Remember your covenant." We have to learn to draw on our suffering, distress and setbacks so that we can grow spiritually. It is so easy for us to get locked into frustration, anger and depression.

* * *

A spiritual counsellor does not always need to give advice. We all have the light of truth in our hearts, and if we are peaceful enough, we will discover the answer within ourselves. But we always need someone who will ask the right questions.

* * *

Some young people who have just had an experience of God and heard an inner call to grow in love may need a very directive shepherd. If their shepherd only asks questions, they will not know how to cope with the experience, because their inner confusion is too great. They will find it impossible to distinguish the dream from reality. If they are to take the first step in inner growth, they need a firm father figure who demands obedience. If they are not obedient, they may very quickly become dispersed. It is up to their spiritual director to be careful that they do not stay too long in obedience; he will help them gradually to trust their own judgement and spiritual discernment.

* * *

Jesus was attacked because he dared to tell people that their sins would be forgiven. The scribes and pharisees said that he was blaspheming. That is why he was crucified.

After his resurrection, he said to the apostles: "Receive the Holy Spirit. If you forgive the sins of any, they are forgiven. If you retain the sins of any, they are retained" (John 20,22-23). The power this gives to priests is astonishing. A lay person can be a spiritual counsellor, but can never tell people, in the name of God, that their sins are forgiven. Jesus came to earth to bring forgiveness and gave priests this marvellous gift of forgiveness in his name. The priest is essential to community life, to help people discover this forgiveness and so to continue in renewed hope. This power of the priest is another reason for him not to hold temporal power in a community.

* * *

Our l'Arche communities are always in need of these priest-shepherds who bring the nourishment of the Eucharist and the gift of forgiveness. We need them both as a community and as individuals; we need to put the secret of our hearts in the heart of God through the priest. But he must be a man of prayer, transparent and gentle, yet firm and sometimes even bold in the struggle against darkness.

* * *

EACH PERSON HAS A GIFT TO SHARE

A community is like an orchestra: each instrument is beautiful when it plays alone, but when they all play together, each given its own weight in turn, the result is even more beautiful. A community is like a garden full of flowers, shrubs and trees. Each helps to give life to the other. Together, they bear witness to the beauty of God, creator and gardener-extraordinary.

* * *

When people are using their gifts, it is important that the community prays for them to be more open to inspiration and more an instrument of God, so that they can use those gifts better. It is important, too, that the community welcomes those gifts in love and gratitude. It should also pray for the people who carry authority and those who inspire through their words. So we participate in each others' gifts, and help each other build community.

* * *

At l'Arche, we need people who are competent teachers and trained workers. We also need people who are open to whatever comes, who live in our houses, love community life and above all want to live with, and discover the gifts of, the handicapped person. We need people who are set in their spiritual and religious life, who spend time with God in prayer. They all bring their own gift, and all these gifts are needed for the building, wellbeing, radiance and unity of the community. We are all indispensible in our own way.

Of course we all have to grow in wholeness, becoming more competent, more open to the demands of community life, closer to the handicapped people and more prayerful. But people will put more of their energy into the exercise of their own particular gift.

* * *

To love people is to recognise their gift and to help them use

154

it and deepen it. A community is beautiful when all its members are using their talents fully.

* * *

"Bear one another's burden and so fulfill the law of Christ" (Galatians 6,2). "The freedom of the other person includes all that we mean by a person's nature, individuality, endowment. It also includes his weaknesses and oddities, which are such a trial to our patience, everything that produces friction, conflicts and collisions among us. To bear the burdens of the other person means involvement with the created reality of the other, to accept and affirm it, and, in bearing with it, to break through to the point where we take joy in it ... The service of forgiveness is rendered by one to the others daily. It occurs, without words, in the intercessions for one another. And every member of the fellowship, who does not grow weary in this ministry, can depend upon it, that this service is also being rendered him by the brethren. He who is bearing others knows that he himself is being borne and only in this strength can he go on bearing."[1]

* * *

The gift of listening

This is an important gift in community. But if we are to be able to listen, we must offer security. None of us would speak to people unless we knew that they were safe and would respect our secret. An assurance of confidentiality is an essential part of being a listener. This means knowing how to respect the wounds and the sufferings of others and not divulging these.

* * *

The gift of discernment

Some people have a true gift of discernment. They can seize what is essential in a complicated discussion or a confused story. They are quick to understand what is really needed and at the same time, if they are practical, they can suggest the first steps toward putting people on the road to healing. Some

[1] Dietrich Bonhoeffer, *Living Together*, Harper & Row, New York, 1954.

people in a community who do not have an important position may have the gift of light for us. We have to learn to listen to them.

* * *

Fidelity over time

A Benedictine abbot once told me how he marvelled at the fidelity of his monks. But, he added, they also needed refreshment and rejuvenation.

At a time when so many new communities are being born, which are sometimes clamourous in their songs, youth and excitement, we should not forget the old communities, which have worked the earth and lived peacefully, in prayer, silence, worship and forgiveness, and whose tradition goes back for centuries. People who are coming into community have a lot to learn from the wisdom of these foundations which are living fidelity without making too much noise about it. Many young communities, with all their enthusiasm and emotionalism, will die, while those which are more silent and serene will continue their journey through the generations.

We who are young in community should beware of believing that we have the only answer and can teach these wise men and women who have so much experience of the human and the divine, and have been walking with Jesus for so many years. They have the gift of fidelity.

* * *

The gift of wonderment

People who have spent a long time in community tend to forget what is beautiful in it. They may be too taken up with immediate needs; they may have got stuck in a rut. They have lost the grace of wonderment. They need to be renewed by listening to the sense of wonder of the younger people who feel called to commit themselves to the community.

The greatest sin of people who have spent a long time in community is to accuse the newcomers of naivete and condemn their enthusiasm and generosity. The sense of wonderment of the young blends with the fidelity, wisdom and ability to listen of the older members to make a community which is really beautiful.

A grandmother is always given new life by her grandchildren. Communities need grandmothers, who may have more time to marvel than other people, because they carry no responsibilities. It is always good when a community has a wide spread of age, from the very young to the very old. The complementarity, as in a family, brings peace. When everyone is the same age, it can be exciting for a time, but weariness soon sets in. We need to refind the gift of youth and the peaceful wisdom of age.

* * *

The gift of the grandmother

A community needs this gift too, especially if their grandmother also has a fund of commonsense. We too often tend to dramatise our weariness and anguish. We weep and forget why we are weeping. We identify with the agony of Christ or with the most disadvantaged of the world. A grandmother who has experience, who is comfortable with herself, knows that what we really need is a week at the seaside. St Theresa of Avila advised her sisters who were going through a bad patch to eat a good steak rather than force themselves to pray. We have to remember that we have a body which has its own laws, and that the physical has its effect on the spiritual. We have to respect our body and its needs, and care for it even more than a craftsman cares for his tools. Our body is more than a tool. It will be resurrected. It is an integral part of our being, of our self.

Grandmothers sense certain things. And there are things which can be confided only to them. They are important to a community.

It is dangerous when people believe themselves to be prophets or put others in that position. The really prophetic people are those who don't know it, but just live and act.

* * *

The gift of diversity

Community brings together people of very different temperaments. Some are organised, quick, precise and efficient; they tend to be defensive and legalistic. Others are open, flexible and love personal contact; they are less efficient—to say the least! Others are shy and tend to become depressed and pessimistic. Others again are extravert, optimistic and even a bit exalted. God calls all these opposites together to create the wealth of the community. It may not be very easy at first. But gradually we discover what a richness it is to live with such a diversity of people.

* * *

L'Arche communities are a great mixture—men and women, single people and married couples. This is precious and even vital. The men and women we welcome sometimes have deep emotional wounds. They need maternal and paternal models or references.

The mixture of people which is increasingly found in communities can bring real growth, but it can also bring difficulties. These arise particularly when people are not sure about their single state. There is the whole question of people who fall in love in community and cannot take the distance they need from each other to see if this is real love, which will lead to marriage, or a love which has grown from their respective loneliness. There are many people who have emotional difficulties because of a lack of love in their own childhood; they can confuse their search for the security of a parent with their search for a husband or wife. The community can help them to integrate their sexuality and find emotional stability, especially if it has very clear and demanding goals, if there is a lot of laughter and if there are well-established traditions on the relationships between men and women.

Communities can be much taken up with questions about what is permitted sexual behaviour and what is not. We forget the fundamental questions: what is the final goal of humanity, what are its essential activities and what is the meaning of human growth? We forget to ask what makes for true growth in love.

* * *

There is a movement today to suppress all the differences between men and women. We seek equality in everything: women want to become priests and men want to stay at home and look after the children. It is certainly still true that men tend to see themselves as superior, powerful, strong and intelligent and tend to relegate women to a subordinate place. There is something shocking about men who spend their time and money in bars while women raise their children. We can understand that when men behave like this, they are trying to prove their virility and putting all their energies into external things—like physical strength and the ability to use this to dominate. Women are often more internalised and, by the fact of child-bearing, much closer to the reality of love and the world of emotions.

But men are in danger of fleeing their own vulnerability and capacity for tenderness. They seek a wife-mother and then, very quickly and like small boys, they reject her because they want their freedom. They will throw themselves into the world of efficiency and organisation and reject tenderness. But in doing that, they will cut themselves off from an essential part of their nature. Then they will either idealise women, as pure virgins, or condemn them as sirens, instruments of the devil and prostitutes. This is a rejection of sexuality, whether it is condemned as wicked or denied. Either way, the man will reject any true relationship with a woman because he can see her only as a symbol of either purity or sin.

A man has to grow into mature relationships with women, to get beyond the stage of mother-child or seduction-revulsion. This means he has to discover his own identity as a man and the dangers inherent in it. He will often need a woman who is comfortable with herself to help him discover his own capacity for tenderness and his own vulnerability, without any threat to his own disturbed and disturbing sexuality. Then he will find a balance between the virility of effective action and power, and his own heart.

Women have to find their balance too. They must neither reject their femininity to seek masculine power, nor envy the masculine capacity for organisation. They have to discover the wealth of their own femininity, the power they have in their weakness and their ability to attract and sometimes seduce men. And in the weakness which comes from their separation from power, women have a clearer and truer intuition, less adulterated with the passions of pride and power which often colour masculine intelligence.

* * *

Men who hold responsibility in their communities can be

jealous of their own vision. There may be women in the community who are more intelligent than they are, more sensitive in their discernment and more sure of their own purpose. The man in charge can reject these women because he feels it would be a sign of weakness to admit that they have a truer vision and greater discernment than he does. The same thing can happen in a marriage. In our civilisation, where the man has to be virile and powerful, there can be a curious struggle between the sexes; a man can be afraid of losing something if he admits that a woman is right. Yet each should be able to recognise the gift of the other. God sometimes gives a man power without the ability to discern and a woman discernment but no power. When men and women refuse to work together, it is chaos. When they do work together, it is community.

* * *

Clearly we can't generalise too much. There is the feminine principle in each man, just as there is the masculine principle in each woman. We are all a mixture of passive and active. But it remains true that their different physiological makeups give men and women particular tendencies: men are more turned towards the external world and women, by the fact of child-bearing, towards relationships. Neither is superior in the heart of God. But women are more sensitive to the realities of community life and men are more sensitive to reason and efficacy. This does not mean that either is necessarily incompetent in the other area. But it is why there has to be cooperation and recognition of the gifts of both sexes.

* * *

The anti-gift

A community is founded on the trust its members have for each other. This trust is very fragile and very weak. There is a place in all our hearts where doubt lives. People who sow discord have a flair for finding that place and feeding the doubt, which is how they can destroy community. And that is an anti-gift!

* * *

I am struck by the people who come into our communities to stay for a time and very quickly put their finger on failings— of which, God knows, there are enough!—without being able to see anything good. They come to see me, to criticise others and suggest solutions. They present their own project—usually involving a particular therapy—and explain how this will resolve the difficulty and put the community or the handicapped people onto the right track. They believe that their gift is to be a saviour.

These saviours certainly have the intelligence to understand and sometimes to exploit the failings of a community. They are attractive; they talk well and they are dangerous because they want to do their own thing. They lack self-confidence and they are deeply unhappy. They need to prove that they exist through their projects and so they tend to be aggressive.

If people come into community in this state of mind, it will be a disaster for them. The right way to come into a community is to feel at ease there, ready to serve with respect for the traditions. A project has to grow in collaboration with others and not as a way of proving that they are incapable.

* * *

The gift of animation

It is always important in a community to have people who have the gift of animating a meeting or celebration. Guy was saying recently that the best way for him to prepare for this was to spend some time before the event, just listening to the inner music and the needs of the people who would be there. Coming with a prepared text doesn't work. We have to be aware all the time of what people are really waiting for and we have to respond to this secret, silent, wish. A talk, like a celebration, must always be a dialogue between the person who is talking or animating and the people who are waiting as the earth waits for water. This doesn't mean leaving everything to intuition. The person who is giving the talk should rather know in advance what people want and what to say. But at the same time, there must be sensitivity to respond to what people really want as this becomes apparent during the meeting.

* * *

The gift of availability

Availability for service is one of the most marvellous gifts that we can find in community. People who have this gift trust those in authority and the community itself, and take on whatever is proposed to them. And if they do not know how to cope, they ask help of the Holy Spirit and of their brothers and sisters.

There is a tendency nowadays to decry obedience, perhaps because authority has been abused in the past. This means that people are more ready to take on positions than to grow spiritually and personally. And it has to be admitted, too, that obedience can be servile and morose.

But it is marvellous for a community to have among its members people with this child-like spirit, who are ready to assume whatever is asked of them. They have confidence that it would not be asked if they were not capable of doing it, by the grace of the Spirit and the trust of their brothers and sisters.

* * *

The gift of the poor

The people with the best sense of what is essential to a community, of what gives and maintains its spirit, are often hidden in very humble manual tasks. They are not taken up with major responsibilities or "important" things, so they have a greater freedom to understand the essential. It is often the poorest person—the one who is ill or old—who is the most prophetic. These people should not be sucked into the structures of the community; that would deflect them from their gift, which is to love and serve. But the people who carry responsibility must know what they think, because it is often they who see with the greatest clarity.

* * *

In a mental hospital, it is often the patients who are the most prophetic people. They, more than anyone, can say what is going badly and who are the good doctors.

Not long ago, in an African country, a religious order sounded out local people to see what they wanted of the missionaries. Should they, for instance, dress like local people and eat local food? The response was immediate. They knew, the local people said, which of the missionaries loved and respected their culture and way of life and which did not. The way they dressed and their eating habits were irrelevant.

162

To know whether a community is faithful to its original vision, ask the insignificant people, those who surround it and are in need. These people know very well if authority is being well used, and if the community is being faithful. This is why we have to pay heed to them. They nearly always have the best answer to the question the community is asking.

* * *

One of the most precious gifts in a community is to be found among the people who cannot assume important responsibilities. They have no ability to organise, inspire, look ahead or command. But they have very sensitive and loving hearts. They can recognise people in difficulty straight away, and with a smile, a look, a flower or a word, make these people feel that they are close to them, carrying their cross with them. These insignificant people are at the heart of the community and carry its extremes as well. They carry the people who are discontent, who are blocked towards each other, who are envious or who disagree radically. It is the love of the hidden people which keeps the community united. The leader brings unity through justice, but these loving people are creators of unity just by being who they are. In their tenderness, they are artisans of peace.

* * *

Many people are good at talking about what they are doing, but in fact do little. Others do a lot but don't talk about it. They are the ones who make a community live.

* * *

There is nothing worse than adulation. It stifles love. It kills people who want a life which is real, made up of gift and loving presence. Adulation is a poison which, if it gets too deep, can make the whole body sick. And to purify it then takes many periods of trial. Flatterers should know this, and stop making others in community suffer! Confirmation of someone's gift is not adulation. Recognition of someone is not flattery. It is good to recognise, encourage and confirm gifts.

* * *

The most precious gift in community is rooted in weakness. It is when we are frail and poor that we need others, that we call them to live and use all their gifts. At the heart of community are always the people who are insignificant, weak and poor. Those who are "useless", either physically or mentally, those who are ill or dying, enter into the mystery of sacrifice. Through their humiliation and the offering of their suffering, they become sources of life for others. "Upon him was the chastisement that made us whole" (Isaiah 53,5). This is a mystery of faith.

At the heart of everything beautiful in a community, there is always a sacrificial lamb, united to the lamb of God.

* * *

In this chapter on gifts, I have concentrated more on authority than on anything else. Other gifts are implicit in other chapters. It is the people who love, forgive and listen who build community. It is those who are sensitive, who serve others, and who nourish and pray for them. And each of us, by the grace that has been given to us, exercises our gifts, according to our own and unique expression of love and tenderness. A community is only really a community when all its members realise how deeply they need the gifts of others, and try to make themselves more transparent, and more faithful in the exercise of their own gift. So a community is built by every one of its members, all in their own way.

* * *

6

WELCOME

One of the marvellous things about community is that it enables us to welcome and help people in a way we couldn't as
individuals. When we pool our strength and share the work
and responsibility, we can welcome many people, even those in
deep distress, and perhaps help them find self-confidence and
inner healing.

* * *

Welcome is one of the signs that a community is alive. To
invite others, whether strangers or visitors, to live with us is a
sign that we aren't afraid, that we have a treasure of truth to
share. If a community is closing its doors, that is a sign that
hearts are closing as well.

But we have to understand what welcome means. Before we
welcome people, we have to exist as a community. When a
community starts, it must be more enclosed, so that its members can get to know each other. The same is true in marriage:
if a husband and wife are constantly inviting friends in, they
will have no time to forge their own unity.

There is a time for everything—a time to build community
and a time to open its doors to others. The second period
doesn't necessarily follow the first: they are bound up in each
other. A community will always need times of intimacy, just as
it will always needs times of openness. If it has only one or the
other, it will die, or at least suffer periods of setback. A community which is constantly welcoming people will soon become
dispersed; it will end up like a railway station where people
just run into each other and part. A community which is

enclosed becomes stifling; it suffers from dissension and envy and ceases to be alive.

A loving community is attractive, and a community which is attractive is by definition welcoming. Life brings new life. There is an extraordinary gratuity in the power of procreation: the way a living being creates other living beings is marvellous, and this is true for the living body which is community.

Love can never be static. A human heart is either progressing or regressing. If it is not becoming more open, it is closing and withering spiritually. A community which refuses to welcome—whether through fear, weariness, insecurity, a desire to cling to comfort, or just because it is fed up with visitors—is dying spiritually.

But there is a time for everything: a time to be and a time to welcome.

* * *

Sometimes when people knock at my door, I ask them in and we talk, but I make it clear to them in a thousand small ways that I am busy, that I have other things to do. The door of my office is open, but the door of my heart is closed. I still have a lot to learn and a long way to go. When we welcome people, we open the door of our heart to them and give them space within it. And if we have other things to do which really can't wait, we should say so—but open our heart all the same.

* * *

Welcoming people means bringing them right into the community. And they, for their part, have to accept and respect the community's goals, spirit, tradition and rules. It is not welcoming to receive just anyone into the community, to let them do anything they like. Some communities start with the idea of opening their doors to all comers. This is simply not possible and only people who have no experience of community life can believe that it is.

When I started l'Arche, I welcomed Raphael and Philippe, who are both mentally handicapped. Several months later, I welcomed Gabriel, a tramp without work. He stayed a few months, but his presence quickly became incompatible with community life. He terrorised Raphael—perhaps because he was jealous of him. If he hadn't left, Raphael would have been in real danger. When we have welcomed people who are weak

166

and without inner structure and made a commitment to them, we cannot then welcome people who seriously threaten their growth. We have no right to accept someone who refuses to accept others or community life with all that it implies.

Each community has its own weakness, its limitations which are also its wealth. It is important to recognise these limitations; we have to know what our norms of welcome are and who can be accepted within them. We can certainly hope that, with time, the community will deepen and so be able to welcome more and more difficult people. But strangely enough, that doesn't always happen. When l'Arche started, we welcomed some people we found very difficult, unstable and violent. With time, they have become more peaceful and found a certain inner harmony. So now it would be unwise to welcome others who could reawaken all their anguish and darkness. We have to respect the rhythm of fragile people who are still finding their own peace and inner healing.

But if we cannot welcome everyone who knocks at our door, we can still welcome their suffering. There is a way of saying "No" which is both truthful and tender.

* * *

Who welcomes?

A leader who welcomes people without living every day with them is imposing his own ideal of welcome on those who live with it; that is not always just. It is the whole community which should decide who is welcomed, because it is the community which has to live with the difficulties as well as the joys this brings.

In l'Arche communities, especially those which have been going for some time, more and more handicapped people are reaching a certain maturity. They have been in the community for a long time, often for longer than the assistants and sometimes longer than the person in charge. It is important to consult these handicapped people before we welcome someone in distress.

* * *

The risk of welcome

It is always a risk to welcome anyone. It is always disturbing.

But didn't Jesus come precisely to disturb our routines, comforts and apathy? We need constant stimulation if we are not to become dependent on security and comfort, if we are to continue to progress from the slavery of sin and egoism towards the promised land of liberation.

To welcome is not primarily to open the doors of our house. It is to open the doors of our heart and become vulnerable. It is a spirit, an inner attitude. It means accepting the others into ourselves, even if this means insecurity. It is to be concerned for others, attentive towards them, and to help them find their place in the community or in life itself. To welcome means even more than to listen.

* * *

Welcome: true and false

The welcome a community offers visitors is an extension of the welcome its members offer each other. If our heart is open to our brothers and sisters, it will also be open to others. But if we are withdrawn from other members of the community, we are likely to close ourselves off from visitors. We may of course—and this does happen—be delighted to use visitors as an excuse to flee from the community. We can get bored with each others' company and so become aggressive; visitors then become a distraction. That can be valuable and even lead to a real step towards the unity of the community. But it is not true welcome. It is sometimes easier to welcome a visitor than to welcome someone with whom we live all the time. It is rather the same as husbands and wives who are always away from home, caught up in a whole variety of Christian good works. They could do better to spend more time at home, being a bit more welcoming there.

* * *

A divided community has no business to welcome people. It would only do them harm. We should put some order into our own house before we invite others into it.

* * *

I'm sometimes worried about the way l'Arche welcomes people. Do we welcome them because we need them to do a specific job, or do we welcome them for themselves, because

Jesus has sent them? "I was a stranger, and you welcomed me."

Of course people have to be able to find their place, and that implies finding a role and a function. They have to be able to use their gifts, too. But we are sometimes in danger of no longer seeing them as people, because we are so glad that a particular job is filled. It is hard to find the balance between using people for the community and leaving them too much space, without a useful role.

* * *

Welcoming Providence

The longer we live in community, the more we realise how central the role of Providence is. Each day we rediscover our own poverty and how necessary Providence is to us. A community can only stay alive when new people arrive and commit themselves to it. What explanation is there for the fact that one person is touched by the community and another isn't? We realise very quickly that people are drawn by something greater than the community itself—a call and gift of God.

And each new person who joins the community brings his or her own qualities, gifts and failings which will, with time, modify the way the community develops and grows. The people we welcome today will commit themselves tomorrow and carry the community the day after that. Welcome is vital for a community. It is a question of life and death.

* * *

First impressions

The first welcome is very often the important one. People can flee because it has put them off. Others stay because of a smile or an initial act of kindness. People should not be made to feel that they are upsetting things when they arrive. They should be able to feel that we are happy to share with them. We have to know how to respond sympathetically to a letter or a phone call, how to add a personal note of gratuity. If we really welcome each new person as a gift of God, and as His messenger, we would be more loving and more open.

* * *

169

Welcoming the vulnerable

When a community welcomes people who have been on the margins of society, things usually go quite well to begin with. Then, for many reasons, these people start to become marginal to the society of the community as well. They throw crises which can be very painful for the community and cause it considerable confusion, because it feels so powerless. The community is then caught in a trap from which it can be hard to escape. But if the crises bring it to a sense of its own poverty, they can also be a grace. There is something prophetic in people who seem marginal and difficult; they force the community to become alert, because what they are demanding is authenticity. Too many communities are founded on dreams and fine words: there is so much talk about love, truth and peace. Marginal people are demanding. Their cries are cries of truth because they sense the emptiness of many of our words; they can see the gap between what we say and what we live. So the community reacts by showing them the door, with all the upheaval that this brings, and calls them unbearable, impossible, lazy and good for nothing. It has to devalue them as far as it can, because they have shown up its hypocrisy.

This doesn't mean that we can welcome everyone, or that there are never times when we should send people away. We have to understand our own limitations and assess objectively what we can and cannot cope with. But sometimes marginal people can become a focus for unity, because they always lead to the absolute. And the absolute leads to conversion. Marginal people can force the community to pull itself together.

* * *

Marginal people in community have very particular needs. They are wounded and lack self-confidence; they are often despairing. They can be buffeted by terrible anguish, which pushes them to attack others or themselves in ways that even they cannot understand. They often lack inner structure and so live in a deep confusion. They can move quickly from a state where they have no desires at all to a state where they are faced with a complete anarchy of competing desires. There is a terrible struggle between darkness and light, life and death.

They have no references, either to people or to laws. And it is their realisation of their loneliness and their poverty that makes them despair.

If they are to refind hope, marginal people have to feel loved and accepted. It is not simply through being welcomed that they will rediscover their own value and capacities for positive action. They need people who will listen to them, with all their wounds and needs, and sense what they really want. This demands time and patience, because they are afraid of revealing themselves and won't open up to just anyone. They need to sense that they are not judged, but really understood. They need someone who can listen to them, a stable reference who can guide and support them and bring them security, who can encourage and help them to discover their abilities and take on responsibilities. Because of their very deep confusion, marginal people have to learn to trust that quasi-paternal or -maternal reference, who unites tenderness, goodness and firmness.

A community which welcomes marginal people has to make clear to them when they arrive exactly what it expects of them. They have to accept its rules, even if these are very flexible and, in a sense, made for marginal people! They have to sense that the community will not let them do exactly as they like, but will demand this minimal conformity. If they refuse this, that is their way of saying that they do not want to stay.

And the people who are their references are intermediaries between them and the law or the rules. They have to explain the reasons for these rules; they have to know how to be firm as well as how to encourage and forgive.

Above all, these references must not set themselves up against the community. Generous people sometimes want to be saviours and show the community that it is neither open nor evangelical. They exploit marginal people to show up the community's failings. People who become references must do so in the name of the community and reflect its wishes. Their task is to help the marginal people progress from this single, individual relationship with them to the demands of relationships with others in the community. This will be gradual. The marginal people will have crises of jealousy; they will test the community to see how far it really accepts them. But eventually, through these crises, they will begin to feel part of the community and at home.

So if a community is to welcome marginal people, it must be able to offer them references which are solid, welcoming, understanding and firm. If it cannot do this, if it doesn't have the people who can accept the occasional blows and crises, it would do better not to welcome marginal people at all. If it is to welcome them, it has to be very deeply united and solidly structured. If this unity is not there, marginal people may well accentuate the tensions and disharmony.

* * *

Marginal people live in darkness, without motivation or hope. They are forced to compensate for their anguish—which can even prevent them from sleeping or eating—in drugs, alcohol or "madness." It takes time for hope to be reborn and for their anguish to be transformed into peace. The rebirth can be very painful for them and for those around them. Sometimes they have to test the community to see if it is really concerned about them. Sometimes they have to unload their personal anguish onto the community, and this anguish can spread like wildfire if it finds inflammable material—just as it can be put out if it runs into people who can assume it. Marginal people are the product of the injustices and violence of their past. Their attitudes are the reflection of these rejections. If they are very sensitive and vulnerable, their wounds will be deep and shown in a confusion, lack of self-confidence and sense of guilt; they can even feel guilty for being alive at all.

Only another person can bring the light which will chase away this darkness. And the struggle with darkness can be a terrible one for marginal people. They are always ambivalent: they vacillate between love of the light and a desire to remain in chaos and tragedy. Their ambivalence spills over onto the community, and especially onto those who are their references —whom they both love and hate. In their insecurity, they want both to become attached to these reference people and to reject them.

The liberation of marginal people from their darkness may mean a long struggle. The reference people and the community have to know how to accept the violence into themselves, so that they can transform it into tenderness and gradually liberate the marginal people from their anguish. The role of a community of reconciliation is to break the cycle of violence and so lead people to peace.

* * *

Many marginal people are in anguish because they have not lived a true relationship with their own mother. This leaves them wounded: they are seeking a relationship of unconditional acceptance. Deep inside, they are crying out for this privileged love. Because they have never had it, they haven't either lived through the normal frustrations of a child whose mother later gives more attention to a new baby. Because they haven't lived through these first jealousies, they haven't integrated them. That is why the thirst of marginal people is insatiable. They want to possess their reference person totally; they refuse to accept that anyone else has any claims. And that is why people who want to help them should never be alone. It is dangerous when a child monopolises its mother's attention, as can happen if she is on her own or emotionally estranged from her husband. The mother and child become emotionally dependent on each other; each possesses the other. Their relationship is no longer liberating. This dangerous sort of relationship can grow in our communities when an assistant concentrates on a handicapped child to the exclusion of all other relationships.

This is why the reference people must depend on the community. And the handicapped children or marginal people must clearly understand that they can never possess these people, whose strength comes from their links with the community.

* * *

Bruno Bettleheim wrote a book called *Love is Not Enough*.[1] He is right—even if he is a bit too analytical in his approach. Here is an important message for anyone who tries to help people in anguish and distress, people who are marginal or living in darkness and confusion. We have to know how to accept crises, violence and depression. We have to understand what people are trying to say through all the re-

[1] The Free Press, New York, 1950.

gression and confusion. We have to be able to decode the messages that are sent through bizarre behaviour and to respond authentically to these cries for help. We have to understand certain laws of human nature and how human beings grow through work and relationships. We have to know how to lead people towards inner healing. We have especially to know how to enter into authentic relationships.

This doesn't mean that we have to become psychiatrists, nor go through analysis. But it does mean being sensitive to the deep needs of other people, being experienced and knowing when we need the professional help of doctors, psychiatrists and different therapists. There is no conflict between faith and psychiatry; there is only conflict between people who deny the value of one or the other. That isn't to say, though, that it is easy to sort out what has to do with the priest and spirituality and what has to do with the psychiatrist; the two areas often overlap.

At l'Arche, we are beginning to discover our own therapy, which is very different from that offered by hospitals or from other therapies based entirely on drugs or analysis. Our therapy is based on authentic relationships lived in community, which bring people hope, self-acceptance and motivation. Through this, people discover gradually that they are part of a family and a community, and this brings them security and peace.

* * *

A Christian community which welcomes people who are on the margins of society and in distress needs professional help from psychologists, psychiatrists and others. But above all, it needs to deepen its own therapy. And professional people have to recognise this therapy and work with it.

* * *

A Christian community is based fundamentally on relationships which are authentic, loving and faithful, and on forgiveness and the signs of that forgiveness. The role of the priest can be essential in leading people towards inner healing. Through confession, and the secret he keeps, he can help people discover the forgiveness of Jesus; this can be central in bringing those in distress to inner healing by lifting the yoke of guilt. The discovery through faith and the love of the com-

174

munity that Jesus loves us all, and especially those in distress, can help people discover their own value as children of God. The way in which a community welcomes the death of a brother can help others overcome their own fear of death. The Eucharist and communal prayer can help us discover that we are all brothers and sisters in Jesus and that in the end, there is no difference between those who are well and those who are sick or disabled. We are all handicapped before God, prisoners of our own egoism. But Jesus has come to heal us, save us and set us free by the gift of his spirit. That is the good news he brings to the poor: we are not alone in our sadness, darkness and loneliness, in our fears and emotional and sexual problems. He loves us and is with us: "Do not be afraid, I am with you."

* * *

When we welcome people who are really wounded, we have to be fully aware of the seriousness of what we are doing. This welcome implies that we accept them as they are, imposing no ideal on them; that we understand what they are seeking in relationships, and that we are ready to "believe all things, hope all things, endure all things" (I Corinthians 13,7).

But at the same time they too must understand the limitations of the community.

Sometimes, even when our welcome has been authentic enough, we find that we cannot keep people, because they are damaging themselves and others. We then have to learn how to be true and firm and at the same time tender and compassionate. If people have to leave, we should try to find them a place which will help them in ways we could not.

* * *

Marginal people within the community

Many communities carry one or two marginal people at their heart—people who, having lived in the community for some time, seem to withdraw into a kind of mental illness. They become bitter, depressed and sullen. It seems impossible to reach them; they reject even the most sensitive approaches. Often when these people were younger, they had the strength to hide their failings. But now, unconscious forces are exploding in them. They are ambivalent: they want to leave the community and at the same time they know that there is nowhere else for them to go. Because they reject all relationships, they feel useless and unloved. They are carrying a terrible cross of loneliness.

The community should sometimes help these people to find a place which will offer them what they need; it should sometimes find them professional help. But above all, it should welcome them as a gift of God. These people who become marginal to their community are often harder to help than those who come from the margins of society outside. But although they are disturbing, they also help the community to be constantly alert to ways of becoming more loving, better at listening and at finding the small things which bring peace. We have to help these marginal people not to feel guilty, and not to withdraw completely into their illness.

The community or its leaders may be partly responsible for this situation. Perhaps they asked too much of these people when they were younger and didn't take enough care of them then; perhaps they didn't confront them when the first signs of their difficulties appeared. If notice had been taken of them earlier, if they hadn't been left alone, there would perhaps have been less suffering later.

* * *

Some people hide their failings behind a mask of efficiency. When we sense this, we have to be careful. Our tendency will be to enable them to go on doing this by emphasising their function. But a time will come when they will no longer be able to hide their failings; they will sense too great a gap between their function and their fragility. Then they may become either deeply depressed or violently aggressive. It is sometimes better to listen to their cries earlier, when there is still time to help them. The most important thing is that we are always authentic and always tell people how we feel towards them.

* * *

Welcome and struggle

Sometimes people get together simply to do battle. They will never form a community—they will remain a militant group.

Community implies not aggression but welcome, trust and openness. That doesn't mean that communities should not sometimes do battle and use their aggression. But the battles have to be in defence of their basic values—welcome and trust.

* * *

Welcome and service

A community has to be careful that it is not welcoming people because this salves its conscience or gives it a sense of "saving" others. It should welcome people because it wants to serve them and to help them find their freedom.

Many welcoming communities want to be Christian communities—which means communities of prayer. A Christian community has to know its own aims and who it is going to welcome. Is it going to give priority to people who are disabled or in distress, or without families, offering them a new family in which they can find greater peace and security and so, perhaps, learn to rejoin society in a really integrated way? Or is it going to give priority to creating a community of prayer, welcoming people who are either Christian already or who will, it hopes, become so?

At l'Arche, we have decided to welcome people because they are in need, whether they are Christian or not. Our aim is to do all we can to help them grow in human and spiritual terms, according to their own rhythm and their own gifts, through the security of relationships. This means that not all our members are necessarily Christian; they do not all join in our prayer. And yet, we are all members of the same family.

The important thing is to know exactly what we want and then to be vulnerable enough to show that we really care for people. This can be terribly disturbing, because we have no firm framework or rules. It is always easier and more comfortable to welcome only the people who come to prayer and Mass! But the danger then is that they feel they will only be able to stay if they pretend to share our faith. It seems preferable to let them discover their own way and the person of Jesus Christ gradually, so that they can decide freely. This way is certainly slower, but because it respects individuals in their own deepest choices and growth, the results will be deeper too.

177

Of course there is always the danger of indifference. But we have to pray that the Spirit will keep us alert to that.

* * *

The need for community

There are so many people who live alone, crushed by their loneliness. It is obvious that too much solitude can drive people off the rails, to depression or alcoholism. More and more people seem to have lost their balance because their family life has been unhappy. There are so many who are lost, taking drugs, turning to delinquency; there are so many who are looking for a family and a meaning to their lives. In the years to come, we are going to need so many small communities which welcome lost and lonely people, offering them a family and a sense of belonging. At other times, Christians who wanted to follow Jesus opened hospitals and schools. Now that there are so many of these, Christians must commit themselves to the new communities of welcome, to live with people who have no other family and to show them that they are loved.

* * *

7

MEETINGS

Coming together to share

If a community is to forge its unity, its members have to be able to meet. When a community is tiny, it is easy for all its members to get together and share—meetings happen spontaneously throughout the day. But when it grows and work increases and there are more and more visitors, there is a danger that the members only meet to organise things. So it is essential to set aside a definite time—a day, an evening each week—when there are no visitors and the community's members can meet among themselves. If they do not have these times for personal contact and some sharing about themselves, they will gradually become remote from, and even strangers to, each other. There will be no real community life. The community will no longer have "one heart, one soul, one spirit."

* * *

Community life implies a personal commitment which is made real in meetings between people. But we are very quick to flee from these meetings. They frighten us, just because they commit us. We flee into administration, law, rules, the search for "objective truth"; we flee into work and activity. We flee from meeting people, but keep on doing things for them. If we are to love, we have to meet.

Creating a community is something different from meeting as individuals. From time to time, all the members of a community should get together and learn more about each other and what they are living.

* * *

It can be hard to share about our life in community. We are very quick to escape into business discussions, or make sure that we have no time to share at a deeper level. But real community sharing has to do with more than teamwork. It implies that we reveal something of ourselves to each other. This doesn't mean a total openness. We all have a secret which only God, our closest friends or our priest knows. Married couples have a secret they do not share with their children or other members of the family. So our meetings are there for us to share what we are living in community. The line that separates our personal secret from what should be shared is, however, a very fine one. That is why some people find it impossible to share at all. Either they reveal everything, using the community almost like a confessional, and almost delighting in their generous audience—which is upsetting to others. Or they close up, unable to talk about anything except externals, because they are afraid of revealing too much. But it is right and good to share where we are in the community, what we are living and how we are reacting to people and events. It is right to become implicated through our words.

It is good to offer a little of ourselves, so that others know what community means to us and what our difficulties are.

It is by knowing each other in this way, with our problems and weaknesses, that we become able to help each other and encourage each other to be faithful. If we are concerned only to show our strength, qualities and successes, we will be admired rather than loved and others will keep their distance. The sharing of weaknesses and difficulties and the request for help and prayer are like cement to the community. They bind people and create unity; they help us discover that we need each other if we are to remain faithful and use our gifts. When we meet at a personal level, and are honest about our failings, words flow spontaneously into the silence which becomes prayer. And from the depths of the silence can spring another prayer, of intercession or of thanksgiving. So we journey towards a community which is one soul, one heart, one spirit and one body.

* * *

Jesus says that when two or three are gathered in his name,

he is among them. Meeting implies a union. Jesus cannot be there if people come together physically but refuse to meet each other.

* * *

Coming together in the spirit

Some l'Arche communities, when there seems to be a complete breakdown in communication, have what they call 'sacred' meetings. These may be held in the chapel—though not necessarily—and start with a prayer and a period of silence. Then people speak, in a sort of discontinued conversation, each in turn saying what they are living and how they perceive community life. It is entirely subjective; there is no discussion or search for objective truth, but simply a statement of what each person is living. The aim of the meeting is to enable each person to know where the others are, and so to meet them at a personal level. The essential element is that people listen sympathetically; there is nothing to attack, defend or reproach each other for. Many blocks among people in community come from the fact that they do not dare express certain feelings— perhaps for fear of being judged. But when they can express them, this brings freedom. There may be no solutions, but at least, when we know what people are experiencing, we can try to modify our own conduct towards them. The simple fact of stating our difficulties or joys can bring us closer together, increase our understanding of each other and strengthen the bonds between us. When we have all had our say, we pray together. And once the meeting is over, we do not return to it. What was said remains hidden in the heart of God.

* * *

The gift of meetings

We do not have meetings either to impose our own ideas or to defend ourselves. That sort of approach doesn't get you far in community. We meet for a very different reason—to hear each other's ideas. The aim is to discover together what has to be done, and that implies that we believe that not one of us is more intelligent than all of us together. That is why everyone, and especially the shyest and least verbal, must have his say.

The foundation of all meetings is listening to the ideas of others.

* * *

It takes time to discover what a gift meetings are, how they help the community and nourish our hearts and intellects. We have to be able to bear a lot of suffering, to go through some hard discussions and even some battles. All that is to be expected, because it takes time for us to let go of our own ideas and projects and to support those of the community instead. It takes time to have confidence in the judgement of others and in the community.

Different sorts of meeting have to be carefully distinguished. We shouldn't expect too much nourishment from one which has to do with administration or with, say, preparing a celebration. Community life means service and these meetings are services we render for the good of the whole. But there can still be a joy and peace in them, if we try to listen to each others' ideas and opinions, and to discover the best way of organising something for the good of us all.

* * *

Each meeting must have clear goals. These will vary and that means that different meetings have to be lived in different ways. Each sort of meeting has its own discipline and ways of participation. According to the type of community, there will be meetings to organise, to pass on information, to share, to discern about important questions and to deepen in community life. Some people enjoy meetings. They find them relaxing —especially if they enable them to escape from the demands of work! Others don't like meetings at all. They find them a waste of time, a contagious disease. Some people come to meetings as consumers, for a nice chat. Others resent being dragged from what they are doing and feel threatened when people listen to what they have to say; their activity motor is revving so fast that they find it hard to sit and relax.

Participation in a meeting means something much deeper than simply knowing how to talk. It is a way of listening, in a real effort to understand what the other is saying. It is knowing when to talk, neither interrupting nor challenging. It is knowing how to refrain from whispering to your neighbour or reading your mail. It is a way of sitting—a whole message of the

182

body which tells people either that they are boring or that they are worth listening to. The quality of attention we bring to meetings and the courtesy with which we listen to people who may be stammering or even talking nonsense, out of sheer nerves, are the best indicators of the quality of our participation. People who are shy and lack confidence can express themselves awkwardly or aggressively. If we listen to them with the same sort of aggression, we can increase their nervousness. If we really welcome what they have to say, we can help them find self-confidence and discover that they really do have something worth saying. If we cannot come to meetings in this frame of mind, they will quickly become heavy. One person will have a lot of difficulty in leading them, while the others vacillate between sanctimonious attention and aggression that shows itself in boredom or anger.

* * *

One of the roles of community is to help all its members express what they are thinking and feeling. It is serious when people feel they have to brood over their frustrations indefinitely instead of talking about them openly. The expression of feelings brings freedom. A community has to be able to listen well enough to allow all its members to find this freedom.

* * *

We should not be surprised if meetings sometimes bring explosions. If people express themselves violently, this is because of an anguish which we should respect. People who shout are not necessarily marginal, revolutionary, cantankerous or destructive. They may feel wronged; they may be going through a difficult time; they may be on the verge of healing or commitment, for this too brings anguish. In any event, they are suffering. If we respond too abruptly, we will not help them to become free and move towards a greater peace and harmony with the life of the community, its structure and its authority.

* * *

Leading a meeting

The first important thing is to start and finish the meeting on time—and that demands its own discipline! It is always good to start with a time of silence, even of prayer, if that is what

183

people want. When there are major decisions to make, it is important to put ourselves before God, so that we can overcome our own ideas, desires and passions. The next important thing is to have a clear agenda, which gives essential questions the time they need and saves us from drowning in long discussions on unimportant details. The leader needs to be firm enough to keep the meeting to the agenda and cut short useless digressions. But it's good to be flexible, too, because sometimes a digression can open up new ideas and help people feel more implicated. We have to know how to seize on these moments, without interrupting the flow of the discussion. It's good too to draw out or create moments of relaxation and laughter. Knowing how to make a meeting interesting and nourishing is an art in itself. It comes with experience and a certain creativity, confidence and humility.

Those of us who lead meetings have to know how to enable everyone to have their say. We have to try to avoid pushing our own ideas. If we do have an opinion, it is better to wait and see if someone else puts the same point, and to encourage them to develop it. There is a danger that it is always the same people who speak—and they are the ones who find it easy. Their interventions can seem useful because they fill the silences and stimulate others. But they can make others aggressive and they are not, either, necessarily the most perceptive nor those who say the most important or interesting things. It is often people who find it hard to talk or who lack self-confidence who do that.

So we have to create structures which encourage everyone to participate, and especially the shy people. Those who have the most light to shed often dare not show it; they are afraid of appearing stupid. They do not recognise their own gift—perhaps because others haven't recognised it either. We have to help those who talk too much to hold their tongues and listen. One way to do this is to ask everyone for their opinion in turn. If there are too many people for this, we can divide them into small groups where they can share more easily. The important thing is that everyone has their say.

* * *

As soon as people set out to prove that they are right or become aggressive because they feel alone or anguished, a meeting is dead. A meeting is only alive when people are together seeking the truth and God's will.

* * *

We shouldn't get discouraged when things go badly and there are tensions. Each of us has to grow, each of us has the right to a bad patch and to weariness, to moments of doubt and confusion. We have to know how to hold on through these difficult times and wait for happier ones. And we have to discover, through difficult meetings, how to defuse the situation, how to meet in a calmer and more joyful way. People with responsibility have to know how to choose the right moment to bring out a good bottle or a delicious cake. These can bring unity too!

* * *

If meetings are well led, if everyone recognises them as a necessary part of community life, respects their discipline and really participates in them, they can become life-giving, times when we are aware of the unity of the community. Then we are really meeting, recognising each other as brothers and sisters and nourishing each other. Then meetings become celebrations, manifestations that we are indeed members of the same body.

* * *

Community discernment

Community discernment is essentially a way of enabling people to overcome their own passions and ideas, and so to understand as clearly as possible the advantages and disadvantages of a particular project or situation. One way to discern is to ask each person in turn to express what they see for and against a proposal, and only then to give their own opinion.

* * *

When the International Council of l'Arche met in February 1977, we decided to hold a large meeting for all the communities fifteen months later. The meeting would be in two parts: the first would bring together directors and delegates from the communities, together with members of their Boards of Directors; the second would bring more participants to join them, including handicapped people. But when the Council met the following September, some people questioned these decisions, and some for good reasons. Instead of saying that the decisions had been made and that was it, we took time to listen to people's disquiet. We started a process of discernment, trying to see as clearly as we could the advantages and disadvantages of the meeting as planned. After several hours, we reaffirmed the original decision.

Seen from the outside and from the standpoint of efficiency, this dialogue and discernment could seem a complete waste of time. But we discovered that it was important. It allowed all of us to clarify our choice, to see the difficulties and even the risks: it created an inner cohesion in the group which had accepted the original decision in a rather superficial way; our confidence in ourselves and each other grew, and this gave the group as a whole greater creativity. Basically, when people have an inner conviction that something is God's will and not just an individual project, they find a new strength, peace and creativity.

It will always take time for every member of a group—and especially the slowest and least alert—to reach a point where they have made a decision of their own.

In *Education for a Critical Consciousness,*[1] Paolo Freiere speaks of time that is "wasted" in dialogue as only apparently wasted. In the long run one has gained a lot in certainty, self-confidence, trust in each other—things which we can never attain when there is a lack of dialogue.

* * *

I'm told that in the villages of Papua New Guinea, nothing is decided until everyone involved agrees—however many hours that takes! It is certainly important to take time to discover everyone's opinion and the deep reasons for disagreement. We really have to examine the advantages and disadvantages of a particular course of action until we arrive at a consensus.

Some communities take no decision until there is unanimous agreement, and if necessary, they fast until they reach it. The principle could be a good one—but some people could find fasting difficult! We have to accept that disagreements exist and that we won't always reach unanimity, however much we'd

[1] Seabury Press, New York, 1973.

like to. Then we have to vote. For important things, a simple majority isn't enough: we at l'Arche take one of 75%. If there is not a substantial majority, it can be better to wait until time has clarified the issue.

We must always pay attention to the minority which disagrees with a decision or is upset by it. This minority can sometimes be prophetic; it can have a presentiment that something isn't right. Perhaps it says so awkwardly and aggressively; perhaps it rejects the decision for reasons which have nothing to do with the particular case but go far deeper and have to do with rejection of structures or authority, or with personal problems. If possible, these deeper reasons for opposition should be brought to the surface. In any case, we should always be attentive to disagreements and give people time to express them in the greatest possible clarity and peace.

* * *

Community is essentially a place of presence. Of course we need words, but it is through our gestures and ways of looking that we communicate loving presence. So meetings need to be seen in their place—they are important but no substitute for love. Intellectuals put too much emphasis on words. They believe that everything can be expressed through them; they want to spend every meeting in discussion and analysis. They have to know how to leave a place for silence and symbolic gesture. Words are there to confirm nonverbal communication, make explicit its message and prolong its effect.

* * *

8

LIVING WITH EVERY DAY

One of the signs that community is alive can be found in material things. Cleanliness, furnishings, the way flowers are arranged and meals prepared, are among the things which reflect the quality of people's hearts. Some people may find material chores irksome; they would prefer to use their time to talk and be with others. They haven't yet realised that the thousand and one small things that have to be done each day, the cycle of dirtying and cleaning, were given by God to enable us to communicate through matter. Cooking and washing floors can become a way of showing our love for others. If we see the humblest task in this light, everything can become communion and so celebration—because it is celebration to be able to give.

It is important too to recognise the humble and material gifts that others bring, and to thank them for them. Recognition of the gifts of others is essential in community. All it takes is a smile and two small words—"Thank you."

When we put love into what we do, it becomes beautiful, and so do the results. There is a lack of love in an ugly community. But the greatest beauty is in simplicity and lack of affectation, where everything is oriented towards a meeting of people among themselves and with God. The way we look after the house and garden shows whether we feel really at home, relaxed and peaceful. The house is the nest; it is like an extension of the body. Sometimes we tend to forget the role of the environment in liberation and inner growth.

* * *

Love doesn't mean doing extraordinary or heroic things. It means knowing how to do ordinary things with tenderness. I find it marvellous that Jesus lived for thirty hidden years in Nazareth with his mother and Joseph. No one yet knew he was the Christ, the son of God. He lived family and community life in humility, according to the Beatitudes. He worked with wood and lived the small happenings of a Jewish community in the love of his Father. It was only after he had lived the good news that he went out to preach it. The second period of his life was the time of struggle, when he tried to get his message across and used signs to confirm his authority. It seems to me that some Christians are in danger of talking too much about things they do not live; they have their theories on what makes for the "good life" without knowing whether it is possible, because they haven't lived it. The hidden life of Jesus is the model for all community life.

The third stage of his life was the one when his friends deserted him, and he was persecuted by people outside his community. People who are committed to a community can also go through this third period.

* * *

A community which has a sense of work done well, quietly and lovingly, humbly and without fuss, can become a community where the presence of God is profoundly lived. All its members will be at home, living all that makes up daily life tenderly and competently. They will be happy to serve, considering others before themselves, communicating peacefully with God, others and nature, and living in God as He does in them. So the community will take on a whole contemplative dimension.

* * *

Spirituality of movement and spirituality of the circle

Some people have a spirituality of movement and hope. They are filled with energy; they are called to travel and carry the good news and do great things for the Kingdom. The spirituality of St Paul and the apostles was of this kind. They were seized by the desire to make Jesus known and to create new Christian communities. The spirituality of others is to stay where they are: it is the "spirituality of the circle." They have more need of a regular rhythm than of constant movement. They use their energies to remain in the presence of God and of their brothers and sisters. Their spirituality is sensitive and compassionate, rooted in the everyday, rather than one which shows itself in action and movement.

People whose spirituality is of the active kind can sometimes be so taken up with the future that they find it hard to live with the present; their heads and hearts can become blinded by projects. If life is too regular, they become impatient; they need adventure and the unexpected. The others, by contrast, become frightened by too much of the unexpected; they need regularity. A community needs dynamic people who construct and do dramatic things. But even more it needs people whose roots are in the spirituality of everyday life.

* * *

It is hard for people who are longing for big things to understand the true human condition: "He has showed you, O man, what is good: and what does the Lord require of you but to do justice, and to love kindness, and to walk humbly with your God?" (Micah 6,8).

* * *

Many people believe that community life is made up of a series of problems to be solved. And consciously or unconsciously, they are waiting for the day when all the tensions, conflicts and problems brought by marginal people and structures will be resolved and there will be no more problems left! But the more we live community life, the more we discover that it is not so much a question of resolving problems as of learning to live with them patiently. Most problems are not resolved. With time, a certain insight and fidelity in listening, they clear up when we least expect them to.

But there will always be others to take their place!

* * *

Very often, we tend to look for "great" moments or beautiful and ecstatic celebrations. We forget that the best nourishment of community life, the one which renews us and opens our hearts, is in all the small gestures of fidelity, tenderness, humility, forgiveness, sensitivity and welcome which make up everyday life. It is these which are at the heart of community and can bring us to a realisation of love. It is they which touch hearts and reveal gifts.

* * *

Laws of matter

There are some fundamental laws which communities have to obey. We have to respect the budget and the system of accounting, and find the resources we need to live. A community needs structures, discipline and a rule, even if this is only to do with the times of meals. We have to know who does what and how. All this makes up the skeleton and flesh of the body which is community. If it is not respected, the community will die. But of course, the administration, budgeting and community structure are only there to allow the community's spirit and goals to develop and deepen.

Some people reject the physical body—whether their own or the community's—as if there were something dirty in it and its instincts were bad. These people don't want structures; they are afraid of them. They reject all rules, discipline and authority. They don't respect the paint on the walls, either. They have no sense of the value of money or of responsibility towards material goods. Their ideal of a community is one which is completely spiritual, made up of love, warm relationships and spontaneity. But they are unrealistic: community is both body and spirit.

If a community can be thrown off course by people who reject the laws of matter, it can also be stifled by those who rely completely on rules, through law, well-run accounts and efficent administration. People who look only to these things kill the community's heart and spirit. As Stephen Verney says, "We are more earthly and more heavenly than we have cared to admit."[1] The same is true of a community. The body is important; it is beautiful and we have to care for it. But we do this for the life, spirit, heart, motivation, hope and growth of those for whom the community exists.

* * *

[1] op. cit. p.8

Love and poverty

The question of poverty is a hard one! A community can so quickly become rich, for the best of all possible reasons. We need a refrigerator so that we can buy meat cheaper and keep the left-overs—and then we need a deep freeze. It's true that a large initial outlay can bring eventual savings. A car is absolutely necessary if we are to shop economically in the market; so we stop walking and using bicycles. Machines help us do things more quickly and efficiently, but they can also destroy some community activities. I would be sad if we ever got a dishwasher for my house in Trosly. If we did, we would no longer get together, relax and laugh over the dishes. Other communities would say that preparing the vegetables offers the same chance to share. Machines can also throw the weakest people out of work and this is sad, because their small contribution to the housework or cooking was their way of giving something to the community. We are in danger of organising community life as if it were a factory—or at least a part of ordinary society. People who can cope do things very quickly with the help of machines; they become tremendously busy, always active, in charge of everyone—a bit like machines themselves. Less capable people are condemned to inactivity and gravitate to the television.

Are there any norms in this question of poverty? One thing is sure—a community which gets richer, lacks for nothing and is completely self-reliant, will become isolated, just because it needs no help. It becomes less attractive. It will be able to do things for its neighbours, but they will be able to offer nothing in return. There will be no exchange or sharing. The community will become the rich cousin. To what will it witness then?

A community which has all it needs and more is in danger of running up expenses. It will be wasteful or abuse what it has. It will lose its respect for material goods. It will lose its creativity with matter and become slipshod. It will become incapable of distinguishing between luxury, what is advisable for its moral and physical wellbeing, and what is absolutely essential. A rich community very quickly loses the dynamic of love.

I remember Brother Andrew of the Missionaries of Charity

talking about Calcutta, where he lived for fourteen years. The scale of human misery there, he said, made it the worst city in the world. But it was also the most beautiful, because it had the most love. When we become rich, we throw up barriers; perhaps we even hire a watchdog to defend our property. Poor people have nothing to defend and often share the little they have.

In a poor community, there is a lot of mutual help and sharing of goods, as well as help from outside. Poverty becomes a cement of unity. This is very striking at l'Arche when we go on pilgrimage together: everyone shares gladly, sometimes contenting themselves with very little. But when we become rich, we become more demanding and difficult: we tend to remain in our own corner, alone and isolated. In poor African villages, people share in mutual support and celebration. In modern cities, they shut themselves up in their own apartments. Because they have all they need, they seem not to need each other. They are self-sufficient. There is no interdependence. There is no love.

* * *

A community which spends a lot of time watching television very quickly loses its sense of creativity, sharing and celebration. People don't meet any more—they are glued to the screen. When people love each other, they are content with very little. When we have light and joy in our hearts, we don't need material wealth. The most loving communities are often the poorest. If our own life is luxurious and wasteful, we can't approach poor people. If we love people, we want to identify with them and share with them.

The important thing is for communities to know what they want to witness to. Poverty is only a means to a witness of love and a way of life.

I very much liked what Nadine said about the l'Arche community in Honduras, Casa Nazareth. There, they have welcomed Lita and Marcia, both of whom are visibly handicapped. They both come from very poor families and it is important that their new home is always open to the neighbours—like the rest of the homes in the area. This is the way that people live there, and Lita and Marcia mustn't live differently, because then it would be like living in an institution;

they need to have friends and live like everyone else. So the local children are always running in and out of the house, laughing, singing, chattering and playing. I asked Nadine if she'd like a tape recorder and she turned it down, because she'd have to keep it locked up to prevent the children playing with it and breaking it. If she did this, a cupboard would become a secret hiding place, and so a barrier to welcome. And then, she said, l'Arche shouldn't have things that the neighbours don't have. If it did, people would want to play with them or have them themselves. So wealth could very quickly throw up barriers of envy, or create a sense of inferiority, because possession means power. Poverty, on the other hand, should mean love and welcome. The question remains the same: do we want to witness to love and welcome, or do we want to retreat behind a barrier of comfort and security?

* * *

But larger and richer communities shouldn't despair! They have to witness to another sort of poverty. They can still avoid luxury and waste; they can, for instance, use their space to welcome more people. Their wealth is a gift of God, but it doesn't belong to them—they are only trustees. They should use this gift to spread the good news of love and sharing.

* * *

Daily rhythm

When I was with Chris, in our community in Kerala in India, I really enjoyed watching the Indian masons who were working on the house. They worked hard, but with a great sense of freedom and relaxation. They seemed to enjoy building something beautiful together—and remunerative, of course! The women laughed as they carried piles of bricks on their heads. In the evening, they must have been tired. But I'm sure they slept with peaceful hearts.

There is something very beautiful in work which is well and precisely done. It is a participation in the activity of God, who makes all things well and wisely, beautiful to the last detail.

In these days of automation, we tend to forget the value of manual work which is well done. There is something contemplative in the craftsman. The real carpenter, who loves his wood and knows his tools, doesn't push himself and doesn't get

194

irritable. He knows what he is doing; every action has its purpose and his work is beautiful.

There is something particularly unified about a community where the work is hard and precisely defined and all the members have their place. Where there is too much luxury and leisure, too much wasted time and imprecision, a community quickly becomes tepid and the cancer of egoism spreads.

* * *

In the community in Kerala, all the water for cooking, washing, drinking and watering the garden has to be drawn from the well. That sort of activity keeps us close to nature and to each other.

* * *

Here's a text I like:

> "For this commandment which I command you this day is not too hard for you, neither is it far off. It is not in heaven, that you should say, 'Who will go up for us to heaven, and bring it to us, that we may hear it and do it?' Neither is it beyond the sea, that you should say, 'Who will go over the sea for us, and bring it to us, that we may hear it and do it?' But the word is very near you; it is in your mouth and in your heart, so that you can do it."

(Deuteronomy 30,11-14)

Daily life in community is not beyond us.

* * *

Life in industrialised countries has become artificial, its patterns far from nature. Houses are full of electric gadgets; leisure activities are limited to television and the cinema; cities are noisy, stifling and polluted; people are exhausted by long hours of travel in subway, train and car—when they aren't equally exhausted by crawling through traffic jams. The films they watch and the news they listen to concentrate on violence. They cannot possibly integrate all that is happening over the world—earthquakes in Guatamala, famine in the Sahel, civil war in Lebanon, disruption in Northern Ireland, censorship of the press, tyranny, torture, people being condemned to prison without trial or psychiatric hospital when they are not ill. It is overwhelming. And people are overwhelmed by it all. They are not equipped to assimilate all this dramatic information. That is why they latch onto new myths which announce the salva-

tion of the world, or rigid sects which claim to have a monopoly of the truth. The more anguish people feel the more they
seek out new saviours—whether these are political, psychiatric,
religious or mystical. Or else they throw everything over in the
race for instant stimulation, wealth and prestige.

Communities are a sign that it is possible to live on a human
scale, even in the present world. They are a sign that we do not
have to be slaves to work, to inhuman economies or to the
stimulations of artificial leisure. A community is essentially a
place where we learn to live at the pace of humanity and
nature. We are part of the earth and we need the heat of the
sun, the water of the sea and the air we breathe. We are part
of nature and its laws are written in our flesh. That doesn't
mean that scientific discoveries aren't useful too. But they have
to be at the service of life, applied to create an environment in
which human beings can truly grow—whether in town or country, middle class areas or slums.

A community should not be primarily a grouping of shock-
troops, commandos or heroes, but a gathering of people who
want to be a sign that it is possible for men to live together,
love each other, celebrate and work for a better world and a
fellowship of peace. A community is a sign that love is possible
in a materialistic world where people so often either ignore or
fight each other. It is a sign that we don't need a lot of money
to be happy—in fact, the opposite. Schumacher's *Small is
Beautiful* gave us a lot to think about.[1] In our l'Arche communities, we have to put still more thought into the quality of
life. We have to learn to live each day and find our own
internal and external rhythms.

* * *

Political dimension of the community

Christian communities cannot be outside society. They are not
bolt-holes for the emotions, offering spiritual drugs to stave off
the sadness of everyday life. They are not places where people
can go to salve their consciences and retreat from reality into a
world of dreams. They are places of resource, which are there
to help people grow towards freedom, so that they can love as

[1] Blond & Briggs Ltd., London 1973.

Jesus loves them. "There is no greater love than to give one's life for one's friends." The message of Jesus is clear. He reprimands the rich and proud and exalts the humble. Christian communities have to be at the heart of society, visible to everyone; they should not hide their light under a bushel. They should be a sign that we don't need artificial stimulants or material goods for our hearts to rejoice at the beauty of those around us and of the universe in which we live, a sign that we can work together to make our neighbourhood, village or city a place of creativity and human growth.

So there is a whole political dimension to Christian communities.

* * *

Some French Christians are very taken up by politics. They can be terribly anti-Communist, forming rather fascist organisations to fight the red devil. Or they can be fiercely anti-capitalist and Marxist, fighting for new structures and redistribution of resources. Both these tendencies can lead to a centralisation—whether to protect the liberal economy or to further wholesale nationalisation.

I sometimes wonder whether these fighting Christians wouldn't do better to put their energies into creating communities which live as far as they can by the charter of the Beatitudes. If they did, they would be able to live by, and measure progress by, other values than those of material success, acquisition of wealth and political struggle. They could become the yeast in the dough of society. They would not change political structures at first. But they would change the hearts and spirits of the people around them, by offering them a glimpse of a new dimension in human life—that of inwardness, love, contemplation, wonderment and sharing. They would introduce people to a place where the weak and poor, far from being pushed aside, are central to their society. My personal hope is that if this spirit of community really spreads, structures will change. Structures are—tyrannies excepted—the mirrors of hearts. But if change is to come, some people should be working now towards a society which is more just, true and sharing, in which communities can take root and shine.

* * *

Communities which live simply and without waste help people to discover a whole new way of life, which demands fewer financial resources but more commitment to relationships. Is there a better way to bridge the gulf which widens daily between rich and poor countries? It is not simply a question of people who are seized with universal love going to work in developing countries. Rich countries themselves have to be awakened to the fact that happiness is not to be found in a frantic search for material goods, but in simple and loving relationships, lived and celebrated in communities which have renounced that search.

* * *

Village people in African and other poor countries have a quality of life. They know how to live in families and communities, even though they don't always know how to act efficiently. I sometimes meet missionaries who know how to do all sorts of things: build schools and hospitals, teach and take care of people. They sometimes even know how to play an effective part in political struggles. But they often do not know how to live together. Their house doesn't feel joyful or alive; it doesn't feel like a community where everyone is relaxed and bound together in deep relationship. That is sad, because Christians should above all bear witness by their lives. That is as important today, when African countries are torn between village traditions and a taste for money and progress, as it has ever been. Missionaries often seem to be saying that successful living depends on being able to use machinery and costly techniques, on having a refrigerator and a car. I always marvel at the Little Sisters of Jesus, the sisters of Mother Theresa, and others who live among their people and bear witness by their lives.

* * *

We sometimes wonder what l'Arche is doing in Calcutta. There are fifteen people at Asha Niketan. Some of them used to live on the streets, destitute because of their mental handicap. The house is in a grossly overcrowded area, stuck on the side of Sealdah—the busiest railway station in the world. Life is happy, through the usual ups and downs. There is enough to eat and there is work from a Philips factory. The community is growing slowly towards financial independence—though it's not certain that it will achieve it. In the street, there is a multitude of poor people who have no work at all. A bit further away, there are some very rich people who seem quite unaware of their responsibilities. So we wonder what l'Arche is doing there—a small drop of water in that vast desert of suffering and misery.

But we have to remind ourselves constantly that we are not saviours. We are simply a tiny sign, among thousands of others, that love is possible, that the world is not condemned to a struggle between oppressors and oppressed, that class and racial warfare is not inevitable. We are a sign that there is hope, because we believe that the Father loves us and sends his Spirit to transform our hearts and lead us from egoism to love, so that we can live everyday life as brothers and sisters.

Sartre is wrong when he says that hell is other people. It is heaven that is other people. They only become hell when we are already locked into our own egoism and darkness. If they are to become heaven, we have to make the slow passage from egoism to love. It is our own hearts and eyes that have to change.

* * *

9

CELEBRATION

At the heart of community: celebration

Forgiveness and celebration are at the heart of community.
These are the two faces of love. Celebration is a communal
experience of joy, a song of thanksgiving. We celebrate the fact
of being together; we give thanks for the gifts we have been
given. Celebration nourishes us, restores hope and brings us
the strength to live with the suffering and difficulties of everyday life. The poorer people are, the more they love to celebrate. The festivals of the poorest people in Africa last for
several days. They use all their savings on huge feasts and
beautiful clothes. They make garlands of flowers and they set
off fireworks—for light and explosions are an integral part of
celebration. These festivals nearly always commemorate a divine or religious event; they are sacred occasions.

Celebrations certainly have a role in helping people to accept the sufferings of everyday life by offering them the chance
to relax and let go. But to see them as nothing but a form of
escapism or drug, is to fail to understand human nature. We
all, and especially if we are poor, live a daily life which brings
its own weariness: we make things dirty, we clean them, we
plough, sow and harvest, and there is no security in any of this.
We need something beyond these limitations. We thirst for a
happiness which seems unattainable on earth; we crave the
infinite, the universal, the eternal—something which gives a
sense to human life and its irksome daily routines. A festival is

a sign of heaven. It symbolises our deepest aspiration—an experience of total communion.

Celebration expresses the true meaning of community in a concrete and tangible way. So it is an essential element in community life. Celebration sweeps away the irritations of daily life; we forget our little quarrels. The aspect of ecstasy in a celebration unites our hearts; a current of life goes through us all. Celebration is a moment of wonder, when the joy of the body and the senses are linked to the joy of the spirit. It unites everything that is most human and most divine in community life. The liturgy of the celebration—which brings together music, dance, song, light and the fruit and flowers of the earth —brings us into communion with God and each other, through prayer, thanksgiving and good food. (And the celebratory meal is important!) The harder and more irksome our daily life, the more our hearts need these moments of celebration and wonder. We need times when we all come together to give thanks, sing, dance and enjoy special meals. Each community, like each people, needs its festival liturgy.

* * *

Celebration is nourishment and resource. It renders present the goals of the community in symbolic form, and so brings hope and a new strength to take up everyday life with more love. Celebration is a sign of the resurrection which gives us strength to carry the cross of each day. There is an intimate bond between celebration and the cross.

* * *

By contrast, there is a sadness about commemorations of political liberation. There is no dancing, no feasting; there are military parades and fly-pasts instead. There is a show of power which people may watch with a certain emotion. But there is no celebration. In France, even in non-Christian quarters, there is a great difference between the tenderness and sweetness of Christmas, when people quite naturally wish each other "Happy Christmas" and the national celebration of the Fourteenth of July, when there is a slightly serious moment at the war memorial, when you salute the Republic—then it's off to the café for a drink. In the old days, people used to dance in the cafés—but they don't even do much of that now.

* * *

Celebration is a time to thank God for an event in the past when He showed His loving presence to humanity itself or the community in particular. It is also a reminder that He is always there, watching over His people and the community, as a loving father watches over His children. We are celebrating not only something which happened in the past, but something which is happening now. For the Jewish people, Passover is a reminder of the time when the angel of Yahweh passed and God freed His people. They give thanks to Yahweh who continues to be their guide, pastor, protector and loving Father.

Each community should celebrate its anniversaries according to its own history and traditions—like the moment God inspired the foundation, or a particular occasion when He protected the community. We give thanks to God and celebrate His gifts. And in doing so, we discover that it is He who is still calling us to live together and work towards the Kingdom.

* * *

The Gospels speak continually of feastdays and celebrations. Jesus's first miracle was at the wedding feast at Cana where he turned water into wine so that the celebration could be more beautiful. It was often at a moment of celebration that Jesus appeared at the Temple and announced the good news in a spectacular way. And he died on the feast of the Passover.

* * *

At the heart of celebration, there are the poor. If the least significant is excluded, it is no longer a celebration. We have to find dances and games in which the children, the old people and the weak can join equally. A celebration must always be a festival of the poor.

* * *

Visitors are often astonished at the joy they sense at l'Arche. Their impression surprises me, too, because I know how much suffering some people are carrying in our communities. I wonder then if all joy doesn't somehow spring from suffering and sacrifice. Can those who live in comfort and security, with all they need, really be joyful? I wonder. But I am sure that poor people can be joyful. At times of celebration, they seem to overcome all their suffering and frustration in an explosion of joy. They shed the burden of daily life and they live a moment of freedom in which their hearts simply bound with joy.

* * *

A wedding is one of the great celebrations. It is a time when all that is most divine seems to meet all that is most human in joy. "The Kingdom of God is like a wedding feast." The celebration is a sign of the eternal celebration. And each small celebration in our communities has to be this sign too.

A celebration is very different from a spectacle, where actors or musicians play to entertain an audience. In a celebraton, we are all actors and all audience. It is not a true celebration unless everyone participates.

But there is always an element of sadness in celebration. We cannot celebrate without alluding to it, because there are people on this earth of ours who are not celebrating, who are despairing, anguished, starving and mourning. That is why all celebration, which is like a great "Alleluia" and song of thanksgiving, should end with a silence in which we remember before God all those who cannot celebrate.

* * *

There are some great festivals which a community celebrates not only for itself but for all humanity. We give thanks together at Christmas for the birth of Jesus, at Easter for his resurrection, and at Pentecost for the coming of the Holy Spirit. Then each community has its own celebrations; the anniversary of its foundation, of its patron saint, the celebration at the end of its year, when it gives thanks for and rejoices in what it has received in the past twelve months. And then there are smaller celebrations—birthdays, weddings, christenings—through which we recognise the uniqueness, the particular place and the gift of each individual. There are also the small daily celebrations which spring up around meals and happen spontaneously when we meet. When the prodigal son returned, his father told the servants: "Bring quickly the best robe, and put it on him; and put a ring on his hand and shoes on his feet; and bring the fatted calf and kill it, and let us eat and make merry; for this my son was dead and is alive again; he was lost and is found" (Luke 15,22-4).

* * *

Each community has its own traditions of celebration. Each has its own liturgy, or special Eucharist, its own way of decorating the chapel. Each has its own special meal and way of serving it and decorating the dining room with candles, garlands and flowers. Each has its own songs, party clothes and dances.

* * *

Rich societies have lost their sense of tradition and so their sense of celebration as well. Celebration is linked to family and religious tradition. As soon as it gets away from this, it tends to become artificial, and people start to need stimulation like alcohol to get it moving. Then it is no longer a celebration. It may be a party, where we come together to eat and drink. These days, we have a sense of party, but when we dance it is usually in couples and often alone. We have become spectators —our society has its theatres, cinemas and television. But it has lost its sense of celebration.

Very often these days we have joy without God or God without joy. That is the result of the Calvinist tradition of God as all powerful and severe, a tradition which separated joy from the divine. But celebration is joy with God. Each culture and each tradition expresses this joy is a different way, with more or less restraint. At l'Arche, we can celebrate with a burst of laughter and song, and then immediately go into prayer and silence. Shouldn't every celebration end in the silent prayer which is the celebration of our personal meeting with God?

* * *

In communities like the l'Arche ones in Africa, where the members come from different cultures, individuals have their own ideas of how leisure time should be spent. Canadians like to have a drink; people from Upper Volta like to visit the neighbours; others want to shut themselves away and read a book. Individuals all have their own preferences. Celebration isn't simply a time for relaxation according to our own culture, a moment "for ourselves." It is a well-prepared meeting of joy and wonderment, which goes beyond cultural differences.

* * *

It is wonderful to see how the Roman Catholic church has kept its sense of celebration. Almost every day is a feast day— either a great liturgical festival or a saint's day. And then at the heart of each day we "celebrate" the Mass. I am always struck by the vocabulary of the Mass: celebration and feast, presence and communion, meal and sacrifice, forgiveness, Eucharist and thanksgiving.

These words sum up community life well. We have to be truly present, in communion with each other because we are in communion with Jesus. And that is feast and celebration. This communion, this celebration, is a time of nourishment. We become bread for each other because God became bread for us; it is a meal at the heart of the community. Sacrifice is always at the centre of community life, because it has to do with the sacrifice of our own interests for those of others, as Jesus sacrificed his life so that we could receive the Spirit. We begin the celebration by asking for forgiveness and we complete it in thanksgiving.

* * *

The Mass is not there just to feed our personal piety. It is celebration and thanksgiving for the whole community, for the whole church and for all humanity. The celebration of the Eucharist is one of the moments in community life when we are most united; everything is offered to the Father in Jesus.

* * *

Meals

Meals are daily celebrations where we meet each other around the same table to be nourished and share in joy. They are a particular delight for the body and the senses. So we shouldn't bolt our food under the pretext of having more important or more spiritual things to do than sit at table. A meal is an important community event which has to be well prepared and fully lived. It is a time when the joy of eating and drinking well merge with the joy of meeting—a marvellous human moment. Meals and love have been linked for us all since we were infants. When a mother feeds her baby, there is mutual presence, joy and play. An infant who is not fed with love and who takes the nipple mechanically, is going to have indigestion. Human beings don't eat like animals, each in their own corner. Friendship and love make the activity human.

This is why meals cannot be times for contentious discussion or serious educational attitudes. Working meals are not to be encouraged either. A meal is a time of relaxation for the body and the spirit. Laughter is excellent for the digestion. Serious discussions cause ulcers and other intestinal problems. Some children really do have terrible problems if they can't eat in an atmosphere of relaxation. I know that tensions at table cut my appetite and go straight to my liver!

* * *

During the course of a meal, each person has to have the chance to meet all the others. Even the simple gesture of passing the potatoes is a natural moment of communication which can bring people out of their isolation. They cannot remain behind the barriers of their depression when they have to ask for the salt. The need for food encourages communication.

Self service is the worst of inventions. There we are, all with our own tray, own little bottle of wine, own little sachets of sugar, salt and pepper. It's like spending every mealtime on an aeroplane. It's terrible to assume that everyone is going to eat and drink a standard quantity, and do it alone into the bargain. How much more human to have a nice big bottle, from which everyone can pour as much as they want, and one nice big dish, so that everyone can make sure that the others have what they need and be willing to offer the best bits to their neighbour. Then meals are no longer a solitary and egoistical business, but a time when each person shares and loves.

* * *

Anyone who runs a house knows that a good meal takes careful preparation—from drawing up the menu, to buying the food, to cooking it, to setting the table and presenting the meal attractively. Everything has to be thought of: the wine, the flowers, who sits next to whom, the way conversations can be encouraged. It is good if people have time to talk to their neighbours. But it is good too to have times when everyone can share in conversations of general interest and laugh together.

* * *

A celebration or other community activity should be at least as carefully prepared as a meal. Things cannot be left to happen spontaneously. A small group of people have to discern the goal and how it is to be reached, for it is within a well-prepared framework that we can best encourage spontaneity and changes in the programme. And we have to know how to capture and prolong the unexpected—the moment of unity, of grace and recollection or of wonder, the times when the current of life is flowing joyfully. If a celebration is not well prepared, you can be sure that either someone will seize the chance to turn the occasion into "their" project and impose their view, put themselves at the heart of the spectacle and collect the applause; or that everything will disperse into boredom, with no sense of unity or celebration at all.

Every community activity should be evaluated afterwards, to see whether we have done what we set out to do. We have to recognise our mistakes and omissions, so that we can do better next time. God gave us intelligence, a memory and an imagination—and we should use them. Americans love evaluating and they sometimes concentrate a bit too heavily on the material aspects, which is why they are good at commerce. The French are not too fond of evaluation. We should always try to evaluate our activities—but qualitatively.

* * *

I think it was St Louis of Gonzaguez who each day prepared funny stories to make his brothers laugh during recreation. He wasn't naturally gifted for this and would perhaps have rather stayed out of the limelight. But for love of his brothers, he tried to inject gaiety into those recreation times. Things can't always be left to spontaneity, because this is often a question of sensitivity or the emotion of the moment.

We have a duty to learn more creative ways of celebrating. We need to find more rousing and funnier songs, stories and snippets of information. If these are well prepared, the meal and other community activities can become moments of sharing, celebration and pooling of knowledge, with all the opening of the spirit that these imply. Too many people come to a meal simply as consumers. They don't realise the role which meals can play in the building of community.

* * *

When we've had oranges for dessert at l'Arche, we sometimes start chucking the peel about at the end of the meal. Everyone gets into it. An Englishman once asked me if this was a traditional French custom. I don't know about that! But I do know that it is one way to bring people out of their isolation to express themselves joyfully—especially if they can't communicate with words. People who cannot participate in interesting conversations can participate through play. When a piece of orange peel arrives on their nose, they are delighted—and they throw it back.

I was once explaining this way of celebrating during a retreat I was giving in New Zealand for superiors of religious orders. The last evening, we had a celebratory meal to which the bishop came. And, by chance, there were oranges for dessert. It was quite something to see these serious and until now rather formal mothers provincial joyfully chucking orange peel about under the astonished gaze of the bishop! He, of course, didn't know how it had all started. There was a bit of explaining to do!

* * *

The way the table is set is important. So is the placing of people around it. If some are a bit strung up, there are others who shouldn't be put next to them. There is a whole discernment of love to be made here. In the same way, when people are sad, we try to make some food they really enjoy. A meal offers the chance of very many gestures of sensitivity and tenderness.

* * *

Eating well doesn't mean eating expensively. There is a lot of good food that is cheap too. It's a question of creativity, of culinary skill, especially with sauces—think of spaghetti without sauce! A sauce is a gesture of gratuity. A community which eats nothing but plain pasta because "it's cheaper to buy in bulk" will never be a very cheerful place.

A silent meal, by candlelight and against a background of good music, can create a very human and community atmosphere. Silent meals are often the rule in monasteries, where people, after all, don't have too much news to share. But silence also encourages reflection and inwardness. And it doesn't exclude sensitive non-verbal communication which can sometimes forge unity more strongly than words.

* * *

Preparing the celebration

Some people refuse to take on the organisation of celebrations "as a job" because they want others to have a chance and because they don't want to be typed as "animators." But if this is their gift, why do they deny it to the community? Perhaps they could teach others how to animate. The same holds true for all the arts—theatre, dance, mine. Every artistic activity can carry a message which can touch people and make their hearts beat in unison. The arts shouldn't be neglected and each community should find its own expression. Every human activity can be put at the service of the divine and of love. We should all exercise our gift to build community.

* * *

Song has a primary importance in community. The members of Bundeena in Australia told me that because some of their people couldn't read, they set some passages of the Bible to music, so that the word of God could penetrate more deeply into people's spirits. St Mary Louise Grignon of Montfort set prayers and hymns to popular music. At l'Arche, it seems to me, we are turning more and more to melancholy songs, perhaps because we want to help people reflect. We need to find some more cheerful ones. There is a whole art in discerning the right song for the right moment: there are some which encourage prayer and reflection, others which encourage us to push ahead. More people in our communities should be thinking about and specialising in this. We too often leave everything to the emotion of the moment. Certainly people shouldn't choose songs just because they like them or they reflect the way they themselves are feeling. We need to find the right song for each occasion.

Wolf Wolfensberger, professor in the division of special education and rehabilitation at Syracuse University, told me recently that he felt we should invent universal dances, easy to learn and perform, and set words to them. In our celebrations, we always dance farandols—but only because we have never learned anything else. There must be some other dances in which handicapped people can join.

* * *

Sometimes we feel we lack a particular gift, because we don't want to push ourselves forward. But we can still ask God to give us gifts, especially if these are to be used to create community. Each aspect of community life is important; some-

209

times we have to work hard to participate in it as fully as possible, and to create the atmosphere of joy and awareness which enables it to flourish.

* * *

In celebrations—and in any community discussions and prayers as well—those who speak must always make sure that everyone can hear and understand what is going on. That means speaking loudly and clearly, for a start. Meetings where people mumble shyly into their beards, so that only their closest neighbours can hear them, are deadly. When we speak in any sort of community meeting, we have to think of the person at the furthest end of the room and, if necessary, stand up. We have to talk simply, thinking of the composition of the audience. It is better to get across one or two ideas that they can grasp easily than to confuse them with a jumble of thoughts that they only half understand. And we have to remember too that what we say is not as important as the faith and enthusiasm with which we say it and touch hearts. It is important that we know how to get across the message we want to communicate.

* * *

Nourishment comes in those moments when the whole community becomes aware of the current of life which flows through it. These are times of grace and gift when the community lives the joy of being together in celebration, feasting and prayer. I remember an evening in one of our communities which had just started. The meal I shared with them was rather sad; each person spoke only to their neighbour and there was no sense of unity round the table. After the meal, we all met in the living room. Someone picked up a guitar and we began to sing. And then, one after another, people began to clap their hands and beat out the rhythm with a glass and spoon, or any improvised instrument they could find. You could feel the current of life! Faces began to light up—it was a moment of grace. We were really together, our hearts, hands and voices beating in unison. But it didn't last. Some of the handicapped people couldn't bear to feel too relaxed and happy; their families' rejection had left them with too much anger. Sometimes we have to wait for a long time for everyone to be able to join a celebration.

* * *

Invited to the Wedding Feast

I have always loved what the King said to his servants in St. Matthew's Gospel: "Go to the thoroughfares and invite to the wedding feast as many as you find" (Matthew 22,9). We are not made to be sad and to work all the time, to do nothing but obey the law and struggle. We are all invited to the wedding feast! Our communities should be signs of joy and celebration. If they are, people will commit themselves with us. Communities which are sad are sterile; they are places of death. Of course our joy on earth is far from complete. But our celebrations are small signs of the eternal celebration, of the wedding feast to which we are all invited.

* * *

CONCLUSION

This book has been about community—community as the place of forgiveness and celebration, growth and liberation. But when all is said and done, each of us, and in the deepest part of our self, has to learn to accept our own essential solitude.

In each of our hearts, there is a wound—the wound of our own loneliness, which hurts at moments of setback and can be even more painful at the time of our death. Death is a passage which cannot be made in community. It has to be made completely alone. And all suffering, sadness and depression is a foretaste of that death, a manifestation of our deep wound which is part of the human condition. Because our hearts thirst for the infinite, they will never be satisfied with the limitations which are always a sign of death. We can touch that infinite in art, music and poetry. We can experience moments of communion and love, of prayer and ecstasy—but they are only moments. We quickly find ourselves back in the incompleteness which is the result of our own limitations and those of others.

We will only find peace when we discover that our setbacks, depression and even our sins can be an offering and a sacrifice, and so open the door to the eternal. We will only find trust when we have accepted our human condition, with all its limitations and contradictions and frantic search for happiness, and when we have discovered that the eternal wedding feast will be waiting for us, like a gift, after our death.

Even the most beautiful community can never heal the wound of loneliness that we carry. It is only when we discover that this loneliness can become sacrament that we touch wisdom, for this sacrament is purification and presence of God. If we stop fleeing from our own solitude, and if we accept our wound, we will discover that this is the way to meet Jesus Christ. It is when we stop fleeing into work and activity, noise and illusion, when we remain conscious of our wound, that we will meet God. He is the Paraclete, the One who responds to our cry, which comes from the darkness of our loneliness.

Those who enter marriage believing that it will slake their thirst for communion and heal their wound will not find happiness. In the same way, those who enter community hoping that it will totally fulfil and heal them, will be disappointed. We will only find the true meaning of marriage or community when we have understood and accepted our wound. It is only when we stand up, with all our failings and sufferings, and try to support others rather than withdraw into ourselves, that we can fully live the life of marriage or community. It is only when we stop seeing others as a refuge that we will become, despite our wound, a source of life and comfort. It is only then that we will discover peace.

Jesus is master of community and it is his teaching which leads to the creation of Christian communities, founded in forgiveness and completed in celebration. But Jesus died abandoned by his friends, crucified on a cross, rejected by society, religious leaders and his own people. Only one person understood and lived that reality: Mary, his mother, who stood at the foot of the cross. This was no longer community. It was a communion which went beyond all community. The master of community even cried: "Lord, Lord, why have you forsaken me?" and "I thirst."

Community life is there to help us not to flee from our deep wound, but to remain with the reality of love. It is there to help us believe that our illusions and egoism will be gradually healed if we become nourishment for others. We are in community for each other, so that all of us can grow and uncover our wound before the infinite, so that Jesus can manifest himself through it.

But we can only accept our own deep wound when we have discovered that community is a place where our heart can put down roots, a place where we are at home. The roots are not there to comfort us or turn us in on ourselves. Quite the opposite: they are there so that each of us can grow and bear fruit for man and for God. We put down roots when we discover the covenant among people who are called to live together, and the covenant with God and with the poor. Community is there not for itself, but for others—the poor, the church and society. It is essentially missionary. It has a message of hope to offer and a love to communicate, especially to those who are poor and in distress. So community has a political aspect.

Community can only truly exist if there is this vital and loving communication between it and the poor, if it is a source for them as they are for it.

So community life takes on a wider meaning. It is lived not only among its own members, but in the larger community of its neighbourhood, with the poor and with all those who want to share its hope. So it becomes a place of reconciliation and forgiveness, where each person feels carried by the others and carries them. It is a place of friendship among those who know that they are weak but know too that they are loved and forgiven. Thus community is the place of celebration.

And celebration is the sign that beyond all the sufferings, purifications and deaths, there is the eternal wedding feast, the great celebration of life with God. It is the sign that there is a personal meeting which will fulfil us, that our thirst for the infinite will be slaked and that the wound of our loneliness will be healed.

Our journey together, our pilgrimage, is worthwhile. There is hope.